Whitestein Series in Software Agent Technologies

Series Editors:
Marius Walliser
Stefan Brantschen
Monique Calisti
Thomas Hempfling

This series reports new developments in agent-based software technologies and agent-oriented software engineering methodologies, with particular emphasis on applications in various scientific and industrial areas. It includes research level monographs, polished notes arising from research and industrial projects, outstanding PhD theses, and proceedings of focused meetings and conferences. The series aims at promoting advanced research as well as at facilitating know-how transfer to industrial use.

About Whitestein Technologies

Whitestein Technologies AG was founded in 1999 with the mission to become a leading provider of advanced software agent technologies, products, solutions, and services for various applications and industries. Whitestein Technologies strongly believes that software agent technologies, in combination with other leading-edge technologies like web services and mobile wireless computing, will enable attractive opportunities for the design and the implementation of a new generation of distributed information systems and network infrastructures.

www.whitestein.com

Nicoleta Neagu

Constraint Satisfaction Techniques for Agent-Based Reasoning

Birkhäuser Verlag
Basel · Boston · Berlin

Author:

Nicoleta Neagu
Whitestein Technologies AG
Pestalozzistrasse 24
CH-8032 Zürich

2000 Mathematical Subject Classification 68T20, 68T35, 68T37, 94A99, 94C99

A CIP catalogue record for this book is available from the
Library of Congress, Washington D.C., USA

Bibliographic information published by Die Deutsche Bibliothek
Die Deutsche Bibliothek lists this publication in the Deutsche Nationalbibliografie;
detailed bibliographic data is available in the Internet at <http://dnb.ddb.de>.

ISBN 3-7643-7217-6 Birkhäuser Verlag, Basel – Boston – Berlin

© 2005 Birkhäuser Verlag, P.O. Box 133, CH-4010 Basel, Switzerland
Part of Springer Science+Business Media
Cover design: Micha Lotrovsky, CH-4106 Therwil, Switzerland
Printed on acid-free paper produced from chlorine-free pulp. TCF∞
Printed in Germany
ISBN-10: 3-7643-7217-6
ISBN-13: 978-3-7643-7217-0

9 8 7 6 5 4 3 2 1

Contents

Preface

An important aspect of multi agent systems are agent reasoning techniques for problem solving, either at the level of a single agent or at the level of distributed collaboration amongst multiple agents.

Constraint Satisfaction Problems (*CSP*) prove to be a generic framework which can be applied for modeling and solving a wide range of combinatorial applications as planning, scheduling and resource sharing in many practical domains such as transportation, production, mass marketing, network management and human resources management. Constraint satisfaction techniques provide efficient algorithms to prune search spaces and it is a paradigm for combinatorial problem solving. As a problem solving technology, constraint satisfaction problems framework is a reasoning technique. In this work we study constraint satisfaction techniques for solving and solution adaptation that can be applied to agent reasoning.

Most work in constraint satisfaction has focused on computing a solution to a given problem. In practice, it often happens that an existing solution needs to be modified to satisfy additional criteria or accommodate changes in the problem. For example, a schedule or plan might have to be adjusted when a resource is missing.

The concept of *interchangeability* characterizes symmetries among the problem entities and thus facilitates making local changes to *CSP* solutions. The first part of this work studies how the concept of interchangeability can define (provide) methods for solution adaptation. In general, interchangeability is only partial and thus localizes changes to sets of variables, which we call *dependent sets*. This study presents concepts for characterizing, and algorithms for computing, partial interchangeability in *CSPs* using the dependent sets. We present novel algorithms for generating the minimal dependent sets for a desired interchangeability, and the minimum thereof. Furthermore we define a new interchangeability concept, *tuple interchangeability*, which characterizes equivalent partial solutions in a *CSP*. We present algorithms for computing this new interchangeability concept and study its dependence on the problem structure. Based on dependent sets and interchangeable tuples, we develop techniques for adapting solutions in applications such as replanning, rescheduling, reconfiguration, etc., which are important techniques for agent-based reasoning.

Classical *CSPs* show limitations in knowledge modeling because they are not flexible enough to model real-life scenarios when the knowledge is neither completely available nor crisp. Moreover, interchangeability for soft *CSPs* is defined and algorithms for its computation are given. We study the occurrence of different forms of interchangeability in soft *CSPs* depending on the problem structure and the relaxation allowed.

Besides applying constraint solving techniques to agent reasoning, another aspect of this research is the study of solution adaptation algorithms based on cooperative agents solving. Search methods are implied for solution adaptation in distributed constraint satisfaction problems where the computational effort can be reduced by the use of multiple agent collaboration. Thus, in distributed environments we show how multi agent systems can collaborate for solving and computing interchangeability of constraint satisfaction problems which are distributed amongst the population.

When the problem knowledge is evolving in time and thus the environment is dynamic we study how and when interchangeability can adapt a solution in order to avoid computation from the scratch.

In the last part, we present another method for agent reasoning based on a *Case Based Reasoning (CBR)* framework. *CBR* can also enrich agent reasoning with learning capabilities. Moreover, we propose a generic framework for case adaptation where the knowledge domain can be represented as constraint satisfaction problems.

Acknowledgements

The research work presented in this book was undergone during my graduate and PhD studies at the Artificial Intelligence Laboratory of the Swiss Federal Institute of Technology of Lausanne (EPFL). The content of this book contains a revised version of the PhD thesis I obtained in EPFL.

I am grateful to Professor Boi Faltings, my academic advisor, for proposing me an exciting theoretical subject that I specially appreciated. I want to thank specially to Professor Berthe Choueirsy for all the precious feedback and deep reading of the thesis. I warmly thank to Stefano Bistarelli with who I had work on interchangeability for soft constraint satisfaction problems, an important part of this book covered in Chapter 3. I want to thank him for all his sustained effort during our collaboration.

I am specially grateful to Monique Calisti, Marius Walliser and Stefan Brantschen for giving me the opportunity to publish this research work and in particular for the chance to join Whitestein Technologies AG. I want also to thank Monique for the possibility of joining Whitestein research group.

I want to thank also to Professor Eugene Freuder for precious discussions, which brought enlightenment to the developing of my thesis, during our meetings in Constraint Programming conferences.

I own a great dept to my family for their support throughout the years. I want to thank Aslan for all the energy, encouragement and enthusiasm and also to all my friends for their sustenance.

Chapter 1

Introduction

In the last three decades *distributed artificial intelligence (DAI)* became an important research area which brings together concepts from many domains including artificial intelligence, computer science, sociology, economics and management science. It is difficult to cover all these *DAI* aspects in a definition, but according to Weiss [100], *DAI* can be characterized as *the study, construction, and application of multi–agent systems, that is systems in which several interacting, intelligent agents pursue some set of goals or perform some set of tasks.*

Based on agent entities, *DAI* systems long–term goal is to to develop mechanisms and methods that enable intelligent agents to interact with the environment or among them as well as humans, and to understand interaction among intelligent entities whether they are computational, human or both.

In general, there is no consensus on a commonly accepted definition of what an agent is and what are, or should be, its main properties. However, the common colloquial understanding is that the term *agent* indicates an entity (person, organization, system, etc.) that acts (1) on behalf of some other entity (an owner), (2) in an autonomous fashion. Thus, an agent is given the mandate to achieve defined goals. To do this, it autonomously selects appropriate actions, depending on the prevailing conditions in the environment, based on its own capabilities and means until it succeeds, fails, needs decisions or new instructions or is stopped by its owner.

A generic definition was given by Wooldridge in [102], with some further adaptation in [61]:

An agent is a computer system that is situated in some environment, and that is capable of autonomous action in this environment in order to meet its design objective.

An important characteristic of a software agent is its ability to interact with other agents. Agent activities can be affected by other agents and perhaps by humans. For consistent interaction between agents, goal and task–oriented coordination methods have been considered. Two types of interaction have been distinguished for agents coordination: cooperation – several agents try to combine their efforts, goals as an entire group and not as individuals, and competition – several agents try to get what only some of them can have. A variety of coordination mechanisms, some of them including explicit exchange of information often given in the form of structured messages, have been proposed in the MAS context, such as organizational structuring, contracting, planning and negotiation techniques[1].

The main focus of in this book is studying collaborative agents coordination for problem solving where the knowledge can be represented as *Constraint Satisfaction Problems (CSPs)*. More precisely, we propose techniques/algorithms based on collaborative multi agent systems for solution adaptation in $CSPs$.

Moreover, an agent acts as an intelligent entity when it manifests flexibility and rationality in various environmental circumstances given its perceptual and effectual equipment. Agent flexibility and reasoning characteristics can be obtained based on techniques such as planning, decision making, problem solving, and learning.

In this book, we investigate mainly problem solving techniques based on constraint satisfaction processing for agent reasoning where we consider the domains which can represent agent knowledge and problems in constraint satisfaction terms. Moreover, we explore problem symmetries in order to adapt already known solutions. Based on these techniques agent reasoning can improve its planning, problem solving or decision making strategies through adaptation of already known solutions.

Constraint networks and constraint satisfaction problems [62] have been studied in Artificial Intelligence since the seventies and proved to be some of the most successful problem–solving paradigms in Artificial Intelligence. Moreover, they provide a generic approach for modeling a wide range of real–world problems.

Symmetry breaking in $CSPs$ has attracted much attention in recent years and has proven to be important for $CSPs$ solving, problem representation, abstraction, or reformulation. We investigate the *interchangeability* concept which characterizes equivalence relations among a problem entities, i.e. one variable values. In general, interchangeability might be only partial and also require changes in values assigned to other variables.

Based on the interchangeability relation we characterize the possibilities for making local changes in CSP solutions. Furthermore, these techniques can be used in solution adaptation for agent reasoning, where the agent has to consider replanning, reconfiguration, decisions remaking, rescheduling, case adaptation etc. in its reasoning process.

When the constraint satisfaction problem is not centralized but distributed in different locations, enhanced techniques of distributed problem solving have to be considered. Distributed constraint satisfaction problems are part of distributed artificial intelligence (DAI) domain. These problems are usually treated when the constraint satisfaction problem has variables, constraints or both distributed

---

[1] For a good survey on coordination in MAS we recommend Chapter 3 of [37].

among a set of independent but communicating agents. We propose algorithms based on collaborative agents for computing problem symmetries characterized by the interchangeability concept. These symmetries can be used for adapting already known solutions of distributed constraint satisfaction problems.

These techniques are also extended to another CSP variant which appears in dynamic environments. In dynamic $CSPs$, variables and constraints may evolve gradually in time. Usually problems and knowledge in multi agent system do not present static characteristics and it is more likely that the information is changing with time. Computation tools for dynamic environments gives more flexibility to agent reasoning. We propose algorithms for computing interchangeability in dynamic environments and furthermore, interchangeability–based algorithms for solution adaptation in dynamic $CSPs$.

In many practical problems, constraints might be violated at a certain cost with the solution being the one with the lowest cost in terms of constraint violations. In some others, preferences might be expressed on constraints or variables values and the solution the one which maximize them over all preferences. For expressing costs and preferences, *constraint optimization problems* ($COPs$), called also *Soft Constraints Satisfaction Problems* ($SCSPs$), might need to be used. In many multi agent systems applications we need to express and optimize cost and preferences. We define interchangeability for soft constraint satisfaction problems and express its use in agent reasoning.

1.1 Constraint Satisfaction Problems and the Interchangeability Concept

Constraint satisfaction is a powerful computational paradigm which proposes techniques to find assignments for problem variables subject to constraints on which only certain combinations of values are acceptable. The success and the increasing application of this paradigm in various domains mainly derive by the fact that many combinatorial problems can be expressed in a natural way as a Constraint Satisfaction Problem (CSP), and can subsequently be solved by applying powerful CSP techniques. Thus, **Constraint Satisfaction Problem** (CSP) framework can be applied to a wide range of problems [49], [40], well known examples are: diagnosis [103], planning [56], scheduling [92], design [45], image understanding [94], robot control [63], and configuration [97].

The literature shows a large variety of algorithms for solving constraint satisfaction problems, and these are applied with great success in practice [93].

In certain settings, it is important not to generate solutions, but to modify an existing solution so that it satisfies additional or revised objectives. Based on the concept of *interchangeability*, we develop methods for solution adaptation.

Interchangeability is an interesting but relatively little explored concept in constraint satisfaction. Interchangeability has mostly been applied as a technique

for enhancing search and backtracking. It has not been effectively exploited as
a technique for updating solutions although it has been the main motivation for
studying it. In this work, we study how interchangeability can be applied for updating solutions by localizing changes in the CSP and identifying the possibilities
it offers for classifying solutions.

In general, interchangeability is only partial, meaning that two values are
symmetric/interchangeable in CSP solutions with possible exceptions in a localized set of variables. We call these *dependent sets* and use them to characterize
partial interchangeability. We study aspects of partial interchangeability, as defined by the dependent sets, in discrete finite constraint satisfaction problems and
their utility in practical applications.

Partial interchangeability has direct applications based on the fact that the
dependent sets determine which other variables may be affected by a local change
to a problem solution. This can be exploited, for example:

- in interactive configuration systems, where it is possible to show what parts
  of a solution might be affected by a local change [97],

- in distributed problem solving, where it is possible to limit the set of agents
  that a change has to be coordinated with, and also to make local changes so
  that they do not spread through the entire problem, as shown by Petcu and
  Faltings [73],

- in constraint–based control systems, where it is possible to choose control
  actions that have effects that are as local as possible,

- in problem abstraction, where a critical variable and the dependent set for
  making its domain interchangeable provide meta–variables, similar to the
  compilation technique in [98].

Problem abstraction and reformulation are fundamental, powerful concepts
in artificial intelligence. As interchangeability is a form of symmetry among variable values in constraint satisfaction problems, it applies and provides a rigorous
approach to problem abstraction and reformulation. Interchangeability techniques
provide methods for operating with compact representation of large sets of solutions. Moreover, by using interchangeability we can permit more efficient solutions solving for the abstracted problem. Finally, these solutions can be expanded
into smaller reformulations of the original problem. In prior work, some forms of
interchangeability such as *neighborhood interchangeability* and *context dependent
interchangeability*, proved to be efficient for problem abstractions and reformulations [25], [43], [95]. Unfortunately these forms of interchangeability are pretty rare
in practice. More tools for abstraction and reformulation can be developed based
on partial interchangeability which occurs more often in constraint satisfaction
problems.

Some of the practical applications where solution adaptation based on interchangeability can be used are enumerated as follows:

- case–based reasoning, where a solution to an earlier problem can be adapted to a new scenario [69],

- rescheduling, where a schedule must be changed to accommodate unforeseen events,

- reconfiguration, where an existing product is to be adapted to different customer needs, see [68] and [97].

- replanning, where a plan has to be adjusted to compensate for a missing resource.

It has been also proven that interchangeability can improve search in constraint problems [5], either as a precomputing technique or during search. Moreover, it has been shown to improve search when all CSP solutions need to be found, as in Choueiry [27].

There is a huge amount of research on searching CSP solutions, but few of them consider the relations between CSP solutions, as in [25] and [99]. This motivates the study of partial interchangeability for classifying solutions.

In many real–life scenarios, standard $CSPs$ prove to be not flexible enough for situations when the information is neither completely available nor crisp. Soft constraint satisfaction problems allow the modeling of constraint satisfaction with preferences, costs, or probabilities. Therefore, there is a need to study interchangeability on Soft $CSPs$ in order to improve solving, reformulation and abstraction of the aforementioned problems. All interchangeability properties from standard $CSPs$ are contained in soft $CSPs$ and due to soft CSP flexibility more flexible forms of interchangeability can also be defined.

1.2 Solution Adaptation Methods and Agent Reasoning

Based on the generality of constraint satisfaction framework for modeling and solving combinatorial problems, interchangeability and solution adaptation become important concepts to be studied. Solving combinatorial problems usually involves a significant computational effort; we study here how and when solution adaptation based on interchangeability can be applied and be more efficient than solving the problem from scratch. Agent reasoning based on constraint satisfaction can be thus improved by applying solution adaptation when tackling rescheduling, replanning, reconfiguration, diagnosis review, case adaptation, etc., problems.

The main foci and contributions of this book are described as follows.

1.2.1 Interchangeability in Crisp $CSPs$

Interchangeability in crisp $CSPs$, where constraints are satisfied or not, has proven to be important for many CSP aspects such as improving search and backtracking in CSP solutions, CSP abstraction and reformulation, interactive problem–

solving and explanation. Much of this work is based on aspects of interchangeability localized to a single CSP variable, with minimal effort in studying partial aspects of interchangeability, which concerns a set of variables. Goals of this research are to define partial interchangeability in standard $CSPs$, to propose algorithms for its computation, and finally to study its occurrence and feasibility in practical applications. Regarding partial interchangeability concept our contributions are:

- We present novel algorithms for generating minimal, and the global minimum, dependent sets for a desired interchangeability.

- We define partial interchangeable solutions, which we called *tuple interchangeability* and give complete algorithms for its computation.

We describe the application of these partial interchangeability algorithms to randomly generated problems in order to study partial interchangeability occurrence and feasibility in practice.

1.2.2 Interchangeability in Soft $CSPs$

Standard $CSPs$ can be often too strict and not convenient for real–life problems. That is why for a decade there has been a huge interest in working on and using Soft $CSPs$ for modeling these problems. Soft $CSPs$ allow the use of preferences, costs or probabilities over the tuples of values.

Our main contributions are:

- We define interchangeability for Soft $CSPs$.

- We propose algorithms for computing interchangeability in Soft $CSPs$.

- We study how soft interchangeability can improve search in Soft $CSPs$.

1.2.3 Interchangeability in Distributed $CSPs$

As the centralization of information might require huge effort for gathering information or may violate privacies, solving distributed constraint satisfaction problems becomes an important research task. A Distributed CSP ($DCSP$) is a CSP in which the variables and constraints are distributed among distinct autonomous *agents* [106]. Each agent has one or multiple variables and tries to determine its/their value/s.

In this research work, we study the following aspects:

- We propose algorithms for computing interchangeability in distributed environments through the use of collaborating agents.

- We adapt the algorithms for computing partial interchangeability to distributed multi agents computation.

1.2.4 Interchangeability in Dynamic *CSPs*

In static *CSPs*, the variables involved in the problem and the constraints between them do not change over time. But this is not the case for real world applications where the variables and constraints may evolve. This type of *CSP* is usually called *Dynamic CSP*. There are many attempts to adopt algorithms from static *CSP* to dynamic *CSP* as well as new methods and approaches. Interchangeability deals with computation of propagation of change through the *CSP* and thus its study in dynamic environments comes as a natural and important research approach. Moreover, multi agent environments are more likely to change with time and thus, agent reasoning necessitates adaptation methods such as interchangeability. We propose algorithms for computing regular and partial interchangeability for dynamic environments.

1.2.5 Case Base Reasoning – Adaptation Process

When agent reasoning cannot be expressed by choice making, other reasoning techniques might be needed. Here we study a recent approach to problem solving and learning that has received a lot of attention over the last few years: *case based reasoning*.

- While there are many general frameworks for indexing and retrieval in *CBR* systems, case adaptation remains a domain–dependent task. We propose here a generic case adaptation method for the domain of problems for which the knowledge can be represented as constraint satisfaction. We apply interchangeability–based methods for updating solutions during adaptation process.

- We extend the framework for case adaptation to *CBR* systems where the knowledge domain can be expressed as Soft *CSPs*.

1.3 Constraint Satisfaction and Agent Reasoning

Solving a problem implies defining and making choices. In this perspective, modeling agent reasoning by making use of *CSP* methods and techniques requires:

- Representing problem solving or agent reasoning options in terms of *choice making* – i.e., identify variables v_1, v_2, ... v_i.

- Gather and process information about possible *choices* – i.e., values variables can possibly take, grouped in domains D_1, D_2, ... D_i – and related *constraints*, where a constraint is defined by a predicate $p_k(v_k1, ..., v_kn)$ that is true if and only if the value assignment of all v_ki satisfies this constraint.

- Access and apply appropriate *problem solving techniques* (many *CSP* algorithms are available) to determine the set of possible combinations of choices by taking into account existing constraints.

The techniques for solving *CSPs* can be subdivided in two main groups: search (e.g., *backtracking* and *iterative*) algorithms and inference (e.g., *consistency*) methods [65]. Consistency algorithms are pre–processing procedures that are invoked before search algorithms. Backtracking methods construct a partial solution (i.e., they assign values to a subset of variables) that satisfies all of the constraints within the subset. This partial solution is expanded by adding new variables one by one. When for one variable, no value satisfies the constraints between the partial solution, the value of the most recently added variable is changed, i.e., backtracked. Iterative methods do not construct partial solutions. In this case, a whole flawed solution is revised by a hill–climbing search. States that can violate some constraints, but in which the number of constraint violations cannot be decreased by changing any single variable value (i.e., local–minima) can be escaped by changing the weight of constraints and/or restarting from another initial state. Iterative improvement is efficient but not complete.

In *CSP* terms, the assignment of one of the values from a domain D_i to a variable v_i corresponds to making a choice. Therefore, if agent reasoning is modeled following a *CSP*–based approach, an agent decision is taken when a choice for an agent's variable is made. Whenever some constraints involve variables controlled by distinct agents, agent–to–agent interactions may need to be triggered. Furthermore, if there are no possible choices to be made within the existing set of constraints, i.e., over–constrained problem, an agent can try to relax some constraints by interacting (e.g., negotiating) with other agents, humans, environments, etc.

As detailed in [21], constraints are used for modeling a description of a desired goal state an agent aims to achieve, and for expressing states of the world involving interdependent choices. In this perspective, an agent's decision making process has been broken down into three main steps: problem modeling, information gathering and combination, and problem solving.

Problem modeling corresponds to identifying the choices to be made, according to the agent's state and its perception of the world's state, which become the variables in the problem formulation. Then it is necessary to identify which options are available for each of the choices – this generates the domains of values for each of the variables, and finally specify how choices are related – generating and collecting the constraints (relations and exclusions) which apply to problem solutions. *Information gathering* and thereby *combination* can involve interaction with other agents. To simplify this step we developed and adopted the Constraint Choice Language [101]. The final choice problem, with all values and constraints gathered, represents a well defined search and solution space. Every valid solution in such space is an acceptable combination of choices (or actions/plans) the agent could make (or execute) according to its goals.

CSPs have established themselves as a powerful formalism for expressing problems involving multiple interdependent choices. Although some experience is required with this domain, modeling agent reasoning in *CSP* terms is in general intuitive and most importantly generates problem descriptions with well defined properties and well studied solution techniques – i.e., many CSP algorithms, techniques, libraries and engines are available and ready to be deployed.

In [64], a constraint–based agent framework is proposed for designing, simulating, building, verifying, optimizing, learning and debugging controllers for agents embedded in an active environment. This framework provides a model for the constraint–based design of embedded intelligent systems, agents, that function in a dynamic, coupled environment. In this model, each agent contains a constraint based controller which communicates with the agent environment through an interface which they call agent body. According to the reports regarding the environment received from the agent body and its internal specified constraints, the controlled based on a constraint solver determines the next agent actions.

An interesting approach combining constraint logic programming and a data model approach, to provide agents with a flexible way to plan and direct their actions and to manipulate and represent its knowledge is described in [22]. The author explores the declarative use of constraints within a BDI Agent framework to represent knowledge as complex quantified constraints and apply these techniques to a courier scenario where cooperating agents communicate, delegate and exchange desires and information using Generalized Partial Global Planning mechanisms to solve a given set of tasks.

However, not always and/or not entirely agent logic can be properly captured and expressed in terms of choice making. For instance, when values to assign to variables are not necessarily known a priori, it may be more opportune to adopt other reasoning approaches, like for instance case–based reasoning techniques [59].

1.4 Outline

In this book we study techniques for agent reasoning mainly based on *constraint satisfaction* methods and *case based reasoning* framework. Whereas both of these techniques provide problem solving capabilities to agent reasoning, case base reasoning also enriches it with learning capabilities.

In the following we outline the main subjects presented in each chapter.

Chapter 2 gives basic and formal definitions for interchangeability in crisp $CSPs$ together with algorithms for its computation. In this chapter we present and discuss also related work of interchangeability in crisp $CSPs$. Furthermore, we study different aspects of partial interchangeability in standard $CSPs$. We present algorithms for computing minimal, and global minimum, dependent set for a given interchange and study their properties and occurrence relatively to the problem structure. Moreover, we define a new form of partial interchangeability which we call *tuple interchangeability*, which characterizes equivalent partial solutions of constraint satisfaction problems. We give polynomial algorithms for its computation, and study their properties relatively to the problem structure.

In Chapter 3, we define and extend various forms of interchangeability from crisp CSP to the Soft CSP framework. We give and extend interchangeability algorithms to Soft $CSPs$. We define two more relaxed forms of interchangeability, which we call α-*interchangeability* and δ-*interchangeability*. We study based on empirical tests how all these forms of interchangeability depend on the problem structure.

Chapter 4 presents formalization of interchangeability algorithms in non-centralized, distributed environments. The computation is realized by collaborative agents.

In Chapter 5, we extend the computation of interchangeability for non-static, dynamic environments where the knowledge of the problem may evolve in time. We study how can interchangeability techniques can help agent reasoning to adapt solutions after the problem slightly change instead to recompute the solution from the scratch.

In Chapter 6, we present a generic tool for case adaptation process in case-based reasoning systems where the knowledge domain can be represented as constraint satisfaction.

Chapter 7 presents conclusions of the research topics addressed in this book and gives further research directions.

Chapter 2

Interchangeability and Solution Adaptation in Crisp $CSPs$

Most work in constraint satisfaction has concentrated on computing a solution to a given problem. In practice, it often happens that an existing solution needs to be modified to satisfy additional criteria or changes in the problem. For example, a schedule or plan might have to be adjusted when a resource is missing. The concept of *interchangeability* characterizes the possibilities for making local changes to CSP solutions.

The main purpose of this research is to define methods for localizing changes in already known solutions in order to reduce further search effort by solution adaptation. Moreover, these methods can provide techniques for classifying solutions.

Basic interchangeability notions and algorithms are given in Section 2.2.

Most of these are motivated by applying interchangeability for a certain goal: in Freuder [5], Haselbock [48], Choueiry and Davis [27], Lal and Choueiry [57] for improving search, in Choueiry [25] for abstraction, in Weigel and Faltings [97] for solution adaptation, etc.

In this work we want to study the concept by itself. We study how this concept characterizes the possibilities for making local changes in CSP solutions, how it characterizes the properties of the solution space aiming classification of solutions, how often it occurs depending on the problem parameters and its applicability in various domains as those enumerated previously.

2.1 Introduction

In previous work *neighborhood interchangeability*, which characterizes equivalence relations among one variable values, was accurately studied and proved to improve search [5], abstractions [25] and solution adaptation [97]. Unfortunately, it occurs mainly in sparse CSP, with CSP density [1] lower than 0.4, as showed by Benson and Freuder [5] and Choueiry et al. [25].

In general, interchangeability tends to be partial in more dense $CSPs$ and thus, requires changing values assigned to other variables. *Partial interchangeability* (PI) was defined by Freuder in [41]. It is a weaker form of interchangeability based on the idea that when a value for a variable X_i changes, values for other variables may also differ among themselves but be interchangeable with respect to the rest of the problem.

A polynomial algorithm for computing *neighborhood partial interchangeability* (NPI) was proposed by Choueiry and Noubir in [28]. It is an algorithm which localizes the change to a set of variables by determining their values which satisfy in the same way the neighborhood of the set and thus, the entire CSP. The problem here consists in choosing the set of variables S on which to apply the algorithm proposed by them for computing NPI and called the *Joint Discrimination Tree* (JDT) algorithm.

In the following, we study algorithms that approximate partial interchangeability (PI). First, we investigate how an exchange of values in one variable requires modifications to the assignments of other variables in order to localize the change. We call this the *dependent set* and give algorithms that compute minimal and the globally minimum dependent set for a desired interchange. We show on randomly generated problems that partial interchangeability tends to be frequent and that the dependent sets are generally of manageable size.

Further, we define and give algorithms for computing interchangeable partial solutions, which we call *interchangeable tuples*. We also study, on randomly generated problems, the occurrence of *tuple interchangeability* depending on the problem structure. We show they are frequent, of manageable size and conclude that they can be useful in practical applications.

2.2   Related Work

The interchangeability concept was defined by Freuder in [41], and characterizes symmetries among the variable values. Freuder introduced a classification of different types of value symmetries in $CSPs$ in [41] under the interchangeability concept, in particular: *full/neighborhood interchangeability* and *partial interchangeability*, categorizes them and gives efficient algorithms for neighborhood interchangeability (NI). This algorithm finds all the equivalence classes of variable values, considering all the constraints of the current variable with the neighborhood.

---

[1]The *density* of binary CSP is defined as the ratio of the number of constraints relatively to the minimum and maximum number of constraints allowed in the given CSP : dens–csp $= \frac{e-e\_min}{e\_max-e\_min}$, where e represents the number of edges in the current CSP, $e\_min = n - 1$ the minimum number of constraints in the CSP, $e\_max = \frac{n(n-1)}{2}$ the maximum number of constraint and n is the size of the problem CSP.

A weaker form of neighborhood interchangeability was proposed by Haselbock in [48]. He proved that the neighborhood interchangeability related to only one constraint can be advantageously exploited in backtracking searches with or without forward checking for finding all the solutions of the CSP. He also showed how to classify solutions according to this kind of interchangeability, and usefulness of interchangeability for arc consistency.

As cited also in [27], various CSP symmetry types with the aim of improving search have been studied by Glaisher [47], Brown et al. [18], Fillmore et al. [39], Puget [74]. They consider exact symmetries specific to a class of problems, i.e. the 'N queens problem' and explore them during search. Later, Ellman [36] proposed to also include necessary and sufficient approximations of symmetry relations.

In its introduction by Freuder [41], interchangeability's main goal was also to improve search of CSP solutions and in this paper it is proved theoretically. Furthermore, it was studied and shown practically by Benson and Freuder in [5] that interchangeability can improve forward checking searches. They apply interchangeability as a preprocessing technique before searching in order to eliminate redundant values.

In search, interchangeability proves to be effective as has been shown by Choueiry and Davis in [27] for finding first solution and in [29] where they prove it theoretically. In [57], Lal and Choueiry prove that dynamic interchangeability during backtrack search for finding first or all solutions is always beneficial.

Interchangeability has been also investigated by Choueiry and Faltings in [25] and [24], Freuder and Sabin in [43], and Weigel and Faltings in [98] for problem abstraction. In [24], Choueiry and Faltings show that interchangeability sets are abstractions of the CSPs, reduce the computational complexity and thus improve the search, and also facilitates the identification of elementary components for interaction with the users. In [98], Weigel and Faltings use techniques which rely on value interchangeability to achieve more compact problem representations.

Weigel and Faltings used interchangeability for compacting solutions in [96], and in [99], they propose methods for classifying solutions based on *context dependent interchangeability*.

In general, interchangeability is only partial and also requires changing values assigned to other variables. This aspect of partial interchangeability has been studied by Choueiry and Noubir in [28] and Neagu and Faltings in [69].

Solution update techniques have been studied also in planning by Nebel and Koehler in [70]. In this study they make a comparative worse–case complexity analysis of plan generation and reuse under different assumptions. Their study reveals that there is not possible to achieve a provable efficiency gain of reuse over generation.

Otherwise, in constraint satisfaction problems some previous research has been shown that there are update techniques which can be more efficient than recomputation of the solution. In [97] and [69] it is shown that interchangeability–based techniques provide efficient and generic methods for case adaptation in configuration. Moreover, in [69] it has been studied how solution adaptation techniques can be applied for case adaptation and can model hidden preferences in a case–based reasoning system.

As already mentioned, interchangeability proved to increase search efficiency in centralized $CSPs$. In the later distributed constraint satisfaction problems studies, it has been shown by Petcu and Faltings [73] that interchangeability techniques can significantly reduce the number of cycles required to solve the problems and thus, to increase search efficiency.

Recently, Hentenryck et al. [50] identify three classes of $CSPs$ that are practically relevant and for which symmetry breaking is tractable in polynomial time and space. These CSP classes present various forms of value interchangeability. Under the assumption that the modelers are aware of the symmetries in their applications, it is shown that symmetry breaking can be performed in constant time and space using dedicated search procedures.

Interchangeability is now also studied for other CSP variations as Soft $CSPs$ [9]. Soft constraint satisfaction framework is a generalization of crisp CSP in which the constraints are not categorical but preferences, costs or probabilities. The Soft CSP is then an optimization problem in the space of all possible instantiations of the CSP variables. Potentially, most real–life problems can be modeled as Soft $CSPs$. In [31] Cooper shows how fuzzy CSP can be reduced to the computation of several CSP and how *neighborhood substitution* in $CSPs$ can be generalized to *fuzzy neighborhood substitution* in Fuzzy $CSPs$, where the aggregation operator is strictly monotonic or idempotent.

2.3   *CSP* and Interchangeability Background

2.3.1   Standard *CSPs* Definitions

Definition 2.1 (*CSP*) A CSP is defined by $P = (X, D, C)$, where $X = \{X_1, X_2, \ldots, X_n\}$ is the set of variables, $D = \{D_{X1}, D_{X2}, \ldots, D_{Xn}\}$ the set of domains (i.e., sets of values) associated with the variables, and C is the set of constraints that apply to the variables in X.

The task is to find an assignment of a value to each variable such that all the constraints are satisfied.

In other words, Constraint Satisfaction Problems ($CSPs$) involve finding values for variables subject to constraints on which combinations of values are permitted. As Bacchus and van Beek proved in [2] that any non–binary constraint satisfaction problem can be transformed to a binary one, without loss of generality in this work, we consider problems which can be modeled as discrete binary $CSPs$. These are problems where each domain contains a finite set of discrete values and constraints are never between more than two variables. In crisp $CSPs$ the constraints are *hard*, where for specific values assigned to the variables involved in the constraint, the constraint is either satisfied or not.

2.3.2 Interchangeability Definitions for crisp *CSPs*

The concept of Interchangeability formalizes equivalence relations among objects, respectively the values of the variables in a *CSP*. According to Freuder [41], the main interchangeability types are defined as follows:

Definition 2.2 (Full Interchangeability – *FI*) [Freuder 1991] Values $X_i = a$ and $X_i = b$ are *fully* interchangeable if for any solution where $X_i = a$, there is an otherwise identical solution where $X_i = b$, and vice versa.

This means that by exchanging values a and b for variable X_i in a given solution, the solution will remain a valid solution of the *CSP* (without requiring changes to the other variable assignments). No efficient general algorithm for computing *FI* values in a *CSP* is known; this might require the computation of all solutions [41].

For more computable approaches some localized interchangeability forms have been defined. *Neighborhood Interchangeability* considers only the constraints involving a certain variable X_i, and is defined as follows:

Definition 2.3 (Neighborhood Interchangeability – *NI*) [Freuder 1991] Two values $X_i = a$ and $X_i = b$ are *neighborhood* interchangeable (*NI*) for variable X_i iff for every constraint C on X_i: $\{i|(a,i)$ satisfies $C\} = \{i|(b,i)$ satisfies $C\}$.

For example, in the problem in Figure 2.1, values r and z of variable X_5 are neighborhood interchangeable (*NI*), as they satisfy in the same way the constraints of X_5 with the neighborhood. Thus, by interchanging r and z for variable X_5 in any solution does not require any changes in any other variable in order to maintain the solution.

NI concept is important because any values that are *NI* are also fully interchangeable. Thus, as *NI* implies *FI*, we can approximate *FI* by just computing the neighborhood interchangeability. Not all *FI* values are detected by *NI*.

FI/NI interchangeability is quite rare in practice. Usually, exchanging values also requires making changes elsewhere in the solution. This concept was defined by Freuder in [41] saying that two values are *partially interchangeable* with respect to a set S of variables, iff any solution involving one implies a solution involving the other with possibly different values for S.

Definition 2.4 (Partial Interchangeability – *PI*) [Freuder 1991] Two values $X_i = a$ and $X_i = b$ are *partially* interchangeable (*PI*) for variable X_i iff any solution involving one implies a solution involving the other with possibly different values in S.

We call X_i *the critical variable*, the set $I = \{a, b\}$ *the interchangeable set* and the set S *the dependent set*.

The example in the Figure 2.1, values w and s for variable X_5 are partially interchangeable with respect to the dependent set of variables $S = \{X_4\}$. Thus, when interchanging values w and s for X_5 necessitates probably changes in variable X_4, in order to remain solution. For example, if variable X_4 has value s when w is interchange with value s for variable X_5, variable X_4 has to change its value as well in order to maintain consistency in constraint with X_5.

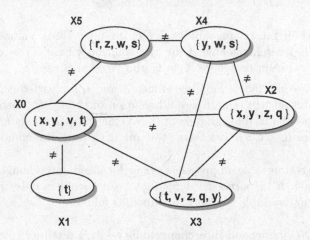

Figure 2.1: Example of a CSP problem.

A localized algorithm for computing PI was proposed by Choueiry and Noubir [28] under the name *neighborhood partial interchangeability (NPI)*. Following the NPI concept proposed by Choueiry and Noubir, we formalize its definition as follows:

Definition 2.5 (Neighborhood Partial Interchangeability – NPI) [Choueiry 1998] Values $X_i = a$ and $X_i = b$ are NPI with respect to a set of variables S if they are NI in the problem where all the variables in S have been removed.

For example in Figure 2.1, we find that the values of the interchangeable set $I = \{z, q\}$ for the critical variable X_3 are *neighborhood partial interchangeable(NPI)* with respect to set $S = \{X_2\}$. This result can be computed using the algorithm based on Joint Discrimination Tree proposed by Choueiry and Noubir in [28].

This neighborhood localized algorithm might not find all the values which are partially interchangeable in the whole problem.

NPI algorithm applies to a set S of CSP variables but there are no specific methods for choosing the set S.

The *set S* in the Definition 2.5 gives the set of variables which have to change so that the solution remain consistent. It is generally interesting to keep it as small as possible. We define:

Definition 2.6 (Dependent Set) The set S of variables in Definition 2.5 is called the *dependent set* of the interchangeability $X_i = a/b$. The set S is a *minimal* dependent set (MDS) if no subset of S is also a dependent set for the same interchangeability. It is a *minimum* dependent set (mDS) if there is no dependent set with a smaller cardinality.

For characterizing the flexibility of making changes to a CSP solution, minimum dependent sets are most useful as they define the variables affected by the change.

2.3.3 Interchangeability Basic Algorithms

In the following we recall the *Neighborhood Interchangeability (NI)* algorithm proposed by Freuder [41].

The NI algorithm computes neighborhood interchangeable values by constructing the so called *Discrimination Tree (DT)* structures for each of the CSP variable. The construction of the DT proceeds in the following way: For each value of the variable, we build a path containing in its nodes consistent values of variables in the neighborhood. Each time we start the process from the root node of the tree. For each neighboring variable value a node is constructed, but in the case it already exists in the next node of the path the algorithm just makes the move to the node. The neighboring variables and their values are processed in lexicographical order. The annotations of the leaves of the DT trees will be the equivalence classes of neighborhood interchangeable values, see Algorithm 1.

In the following, we give formal definitions for the discrimination tree structure.

Definition 2.7 (Assignments) We define as *assignments* the variable/value combinations in the branches of the Discrimination Tree. The set of *compatible assignments* for a leaf of the DT is the set of assignments on the path from the root node to the leaf.

Definition 2.8 (Annotations) Annotations of a leaf node are the variable/value assignments for the critical variable or variables in the dependent set that are consistent with all the compatible assignments of the leaf node.

For example, in Figure 2.2, we construct the DT for critical variable X_5 of the CSP in Figure 2.1. Values r and z reach the annotation of the same branch; it means that they are compatible with the same assignments in the neighborhood of X_5 and thus, they are NI. In the right side of Figure 2.2, we construct the DT for variable X_3 and its values t and v from the problem in Figure 2.1. Here, the branch assignments contain variable/values pairs of neighboring variables X_0, X_2 and X_4 of the CSP where as values t and v end up in different branch annotations.

The Neighborhood Interchangeability (NI) algorithm is computable in polynomial time and approximates FI. This algorithm localizes the search to the

---

Algorithm 1: Discrimination Tree (DT)
Input : X_i

1:   Create the root of the Discrimination Tree.
2:   **for** value $v_i \in D_{Xi}$ **do**
3:      **for** variable $X_j \in$ Neighbors(X_i) **do**
4:         **for** value $v_j \in D_{Xj}$ which is consistent with v_i for X_i do **do**
5:            **if** there is a child node corresponding to '$X_j = v_j$' **then**
6:               Then move to it,
7:            **else**
8:               Construct such a node and move to it.
9:      Add 'X_i, v_i' to annotation of the node (or root).
10:    Go back to the root of the discrimination tree.

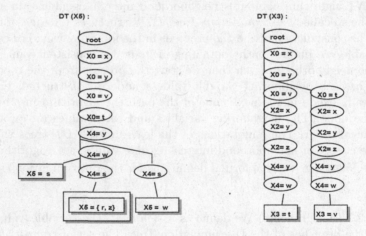

Figure 2.2: Discrimination Trees (DT) for variables X_5 and X_3 of the CSP problem from Figure 2.1.

neighborhood of one CSP variable. NI is a sufficient but not a necessary condition for FI [41].

Neighborhood partial interchangeability (NPI) proposed by Choueiry and oubir in [28] can approximate PI. The NPI algorithm is also a constructive method based on a data structure called a *Joint Discrimination Tree (JDT)*. NPI has as input a set S of variables and has to identify how variables in S (when considered together and regardless of the constraints that apply among them) interact through their neighborhood $N(S)$ with the rest of the CSP. $N(S)$ are all the variables not in S but connected to at least one variable in S by a constraint. JDT is constructed in a similar manner as DT where the branches of the tree are parsed with all the values of variables in the input set S and the assignments in the branched contain variable/value pairs of neighbors of S. The nodes of the JDT contain neighborhood variable/value pairs and the annotations of each branch contain value combinations of variables of S, which represent equivalence classes of interchangeability (neighborhood or partial). The tree is constructed starting from a root node and continuing with branches containing nodes with neighborhood variable/value pairs. All the variable/value pairs of the set S are considering the same JDT starting from the root node. These branches are constructed either by creating nodes which contain neighborhood variable/values pairs consistent with them or by moving to those nodes if they already exist, see Algorithm 2.

Algorithm 2: Joint Discrimination Tree (JDT)
Input : S= $\{X_1, X_2, \ldots, X_k\}$

1: Create the root of the Joint Discrimination Tree.
2: **for** variable $X_i \in$ S **do**
3: · **for** value $v_{il} \in D_{Xi}$ **do**
4:      **for** variable variable $X_j \in$ Neigh(S) **do**
5:          **for** value value $v_{jk} \in D_{Xj}$ consistent with v_{il} **do**
6:              **if** there is a child node corresponding to '$X_j = v_{jk}$' **then**
7:                  Then move to it,
8:              **else**
9:                  Construct such a node and move to it.
10:     Add 'X_i, v_{il}' to annotation of the node (or root).
11:     Go back to the root of the discrimination tree.

Without loss of generality, variables and values are ordered in a canonical way (lexicographic for example). The values of variables in S which arrive at the same branch annotation of the tree have the same consistencies with the neighborhood. Thus, they form a class of equivalence, where by interchanging these values the neighborhood is not affected. These values determine *neighborhood partial sets*.

Complexity of DT and JDT Algorithms

As in [41], the complexity bound of the DT algorithm can be found by assigning a worst case bound to each repeated loop. In the worst case the constraint network is complete. So, for n variables with maximum domain size d, we have the bound $O(n \cdot d \cdot (n-1) \cdot d) = O(n^2 \cdot d^2)$.

As shown in [28], the complexity for computing the JDT for a set of variables S of size s, the time complexity of the JDT algorithm is $O(s(n-s) \cdot d^2)$, where n is the size of the CSP [2] and d is the maximum domain size of variables. Moreover, the space complexity is $O((n-s) \cdot d)$.

---

[2]In the worse case the neighborhood of S is the whole rest of the CSP, thus $n - s$.

Some important results

Benson and Freuder in [5], and Choueiry et al. in [25] found that there is high occurrence of neighborhood interchangeability in sparse CSP, where CSP density is smaller than 0.4. An accurate study of evaluation of NI sets has been completed by Choueiry, Faltings and Weigel in [25]. This study measured the occurrence of NI sets depending on the configuration of the CSP and found that:

- Only problems with low density allow NI values; the number of NI values become near to 0 for a density higher than 0.4 (this is in agreement with Benson and Freuder's results in [5]).

- For problems with low density the number of NI values increases with the domains sizes.

- In general, the number of NI values decreases with the size of the problem.

2.4 Our Contributions to the Related Work

In Figure 2.3, we present our contribution relative to the related work.

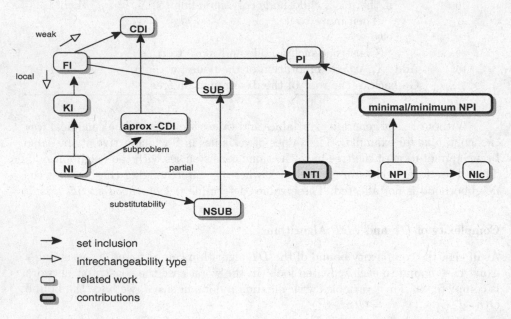

Figure 2.3: Situating our contributions on standard $CSPs$ with respect to previously known interchangeability relations. Lattice extended from [28].

The lattice in the Figure 2.3 was initially designed by Choueiry and Noubir in [28] and describes relations among different interchangeability types. The nodes represent various interchangeability forms and the directed edges indicate a set inclusion relation between these sets.

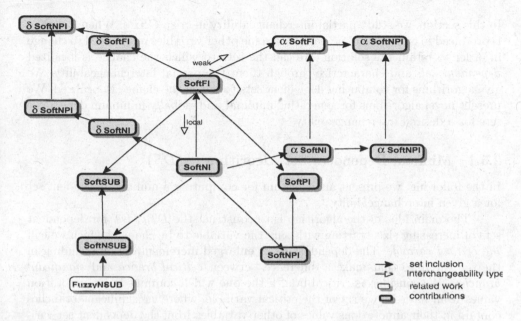

Figure 2.4: Contributions in Soft *CSPs*.

As we can see in Figure 2.3, our main contribution is the definition of a new type of interchangeability called *neighborhood tuple interchangeability (NTI)*.

NTI is a form of partial interchangeability that approximates *partial interchangeability (PI)* in *CSPs*.

Based on *NPI* we give algorithms for finding minimal dependent sets for a given interchange. These dependent sets allow for finding partial interchangeable values.

In Figure 2.4, we present a similar lattice for different forms of interchangeability and their relations in the Soft *CSP* framework. We have extended almost all the forms of interchangeability from crisp *CSPs* to the Soft *CSPs* framework.

Moreover, as Soft *CSPs* is a more flexible framework than standard *CSP*, it allows for more relaxed forms of interchangeability. We define two novel interchangeability forms which we call *α–interchangeability* and *δ–interchangeability*, see Figure 2.4.

Definitions for values substitution in Fuzzy *CSPs* were given in [31]. As Fuzzy *CSP* is an instance of Soft *CSPs*, we consider definitions of Soft *CSP* substitutability more general, see Figure 2.4.

2.5   Partial Interchangeability – Minimal/Minimum Dependent Sets

In this section, we study partial interchangeability in crisp $CSPs$. When a change is produced in one of the CSP variables, some other variables might need to change in order to retain the solution. We call the sets to which the change is localized *dependent sets* and characterize through them the partial interchangeability. We give algorithms for computing dependent sets to which the change is localized. We present novel algorithms for generating minimal and globally minimum dependent sets for a desired interchangeability.

2.5.1   Minimal Dependent Set Algorithm (MDS)

In the following, we present an algorithm for computing a minimal dependent set for a given interchangeability.

The main idea of the algorithm is to construct the DT/JDT for dependent sets of increasing size, starting with only the variable to be changed which we call *the critical variable*. The dependent set is enlarged incrementally by including in the set variables that make a difference between *critical branch* and *significant branches*. We consider as critical branch the one which contains in its annotation values from interchange set of the critical variable, where as significant branches contain in their annotations values of other variables from the dependent set variables.

So, the basic method is as follows:

1. Start by constructing the Discrimination Tree (DT) of the critical variable X_i and its values to interchange, $I = \{v_1, v_2\}$.

2. If the values v_1 and v_2 are not in the annotation of the same branch, we reconstruct the JDT of the set formed by the starting variable X_i and the variables found to make the difference between the branches which contain values v_1 and v_2 in their annotation. [3] Thus, $S_i = X_i \cup DifferenceVars$. We call the annotation containing the values v_1 and v_2 the *critical annotation*, and its branch *critical branch*.

3. Check if the actual JDT contains values in the critical annotation for each variable from S for which the JDT was constructed.

4. If this is not the case, we try further to reconstruct the JDT for a new set S_j which includes the former S_i and the variables which make the difference between the critical branch and a selected branch containing in its annotation values for variables missing in the critical annotation.

---

[3] Note that in the next JDT the values v_1 and v_2 of variable X_i will join the same annotation as we eliminate from the neighboring those variables which make the difference between their branches in the DT tree.

We have the following heuristic for choosing between branches: the algorithm selects the branch with the smallest difference in assignments relatively to the critical branch and containing in its annotation the highest number of values for variables missing in the critical annotation.

5. The operation is reiterated until the critical annotation contains values for all variables of the current S. These values of the critical annotation represents the *minimal dependent set (MDS)* and the algorithm returns it.

Simply put, the basic principle is the following: whenever two values are not values, we see where the branches assignments differ in terms of variables. Those variables should be included in the set S (and thus take out of the tree) and the iteration restarts by the construction of the JDT of the new set S, until the critical annotation contains all the values to interchange of the critical variable and at least one value for each variable of the dependent set.

The algorithm can be extended in a straightforward manner for an input set of critical variables with their corresponding interchangeable sets in order to identify one MDS set. The generalization is obtained by starting the algorithm from step 2.

In the algorithm, the idea remains the same: we try to bring in the annotation of the critical branch all the variables from the input with the corresponding interchangeable sets by including in the set the variables which make the difference between the branches.

The output of MDS algorithm is a MDS set which contains the set of CSP variables to which the change is localizes and their corresponding domain partitions which characterize the PI values.

Minimal Dependent Set (MDS) set characteristics

A generic MDS set is characterized by a set $S = \{X_i, X_j, X_k\}$ of CSP variables, and the corresponding PI values $PI(S) = \{(X_i, \{v_{i1}, v_{i2}\}), (X_j, \{v_{j1}, v_{j2}, \dots\}), (X_k, \{v_{k1}, v_{k2}, \dots\})\}$
The MDS set characteristics are as follows:

1. MDS contains the critical variable X_i and its values to be interchanged from the set I.

2. The MDS set is obtained by applying iteratively the JDT algorithm on an gradually increasing set S until each variables in S reach the critical annotation, where the critical variable contains the values to interchange.

3. The branch, which has MDS in its annotation, contains all the neighbor variables with at least one value; otherwise this MDS set is not of interest as it means that there is no solution for the CSP.

4. The variables in a MDS set have to be a connected graph. We explain this MDS as follows: Suppose variable $X_k \in S$ has no constraints with any of

the other two variables. As there are no constraints that means that all the values of X_i and X_j are compatible with all the values of X_k. That means that there exists NPI values for the set S'=$\{X_i, X_j\} \in S$. That proves that S is not a MDS set for the values v_{i1}, v_{i2} of the variable X_i.

The MDS algorithm has as input the critical variable X_i and the interchangeable set $I = \{v_1, v_2\}$ which contains the values to interchange, see Algorithm 3.

Algorithm 3: Algorithm for Searching a Minimal Dependent Set (MDS), Input: $\{\{X_i\}, I = \{v_1, v_2\}\}$

1:   $S \leftarrow \{X_i\}$.
2:   Construct the $DT(X_i)$ for values in I.
3:   **if** DT Branches contain all the neighbors of X_i **then**
4:       **if** v_1 and v_2 in different annotations **then**
5:           $S \leftarrow$ insert variables which make the differences between the branches having in their annotations v_1 and v_2.
6:           $MDS \leftarrow$ Algorithm4: Heuristic1(S, X_i, I).
7:       **else**
8:           $MDS \leftarrow \{X_i\}$ /* values v_1, v_2 are NI */.
9:   **else**
10:      MDS is null.
11: **return** MDS set for variable X_i and values in I.

Algorithm 3 tests first if values in the interchangeable set I are NI [4]. If not, it continues to further search for the set S formed by the critical variable and the variables which are making the difference between the $DT(X_i)$ branches.

Algorithm 3 also checks if all the neighbors of the critical variable occur in the branches of the values to interchange in the set I. We call here *critical branches* the DT branches containing in their annotations values of the interchangeable set I. This is important as:

Lemma 2.1
If critical branches of the DT of the critical variable X_i do not contain all the variables in the neighborhood of the critical variable X_i than there is no guarantee for valid solutions in which to exchange values of the interchangeable set I.

Proof. If a neighbor variable X_{nj} of the critical variable X_i is missing from one of the critical branches, then the value to interchange $v_j \in I$ contained in the annotation of this branch do not have any consistency with the neighbor missing in the branch. So, this value does not appear in any solution and it is therefore not worth continuing search for the minimal set for it.   □

---

[4]In the first step we construct a DT as in the input we have initially only one variable. We show further that the Algorithm 3 is extendable in a straightforward manner for an input containing a set of variables and their corresponding interchangeable sets.

Theorem 2.1
A critical branch of a $JDT(S)$ contains values for all the variables in the neighborhood of S.

Proof. According to Lemma 2.1, the search for MDS set proceeds by Algorithm 3 and is continued only when all the variables in the neighborhood of the critical variable have consistencies with values in set I. And as for all the other neighbors of the set S, the critical variable has universal constraints [5], the critical branch contains values for all the variables in the neighborhood of S.   □

After checking that the critical branches contain at all variables in the neighborhood and that the values to interchange are not in the same annotation, Algorithm 3 proceeds to step 5 and computes the differences between the critical branches in order to obtain the variables that make difference for the values to interchange. The comparison between the critical branches is simply a vectors comparison, whose elements consist in vectors of values for each variable in the neighborhood.

In step 6 of Algorithm 3, further search for an MDS set can be continued by heuristic search, see Algorithm 4 or Algorithm 5. We propose two heuristic search procedures: one proceeds to search on the branch with minimal difference in assignments relative to the critical branch and the second proceeds to search by backtracking to other branches alternatives when a MDS set is not found during previous searches.

Algorithm 4 searches through the $JDT(S)$ in the following way: When variables from S are missing in the critical annotation, A, it chooses one branch among those having minimum differences relative to the critical branch and containing in its annotation variable X_k missing in A [6]. The search is continued iteratively in the same way until we obtain a critical annotation that contains all the variables from the set S.

Algorithm 4 is sound as it guarantees to return an MDS set satisfying all the characteristics, in Section 2.5.1, and is complete in the sense that it returns one of the MDS sets.

Algorithm 5 proceeds with a more exhaustive search than Algorithm 4 in the sense that it is backtracking on other minimum difference branches alternatives when an MDS is not found for the current branch [7]. By backtracking on other branches with minimum difference to the critical branch at one level, we might find a smaller MDS than in the case where we continue to search on only one alternative. So, we can use $Heuristic2$ as described in Algorithm 5 instead of Algorithm 4. Also, when an MDS is not found in any of the alternatives at

---

[5] A universal constraint is when values of one variable are compatible with the entire domain of another, as in Choueiry and Noubir [28].

[6] Variable X_k is chosen in the lexicographical order among those missing from the critical annotation A

[7] MDS is not found when not all the variables from the set S for which the JDT was constructed do not reach the critical annotation.

Algorithm 4: Heuristic1 (with heuristic search for choosing minimum difference branch)

Input: $\{\{S\}, \{X_i\}, I = \{v_1, v_2\}\}$

1: **repeat**
2:     Construct $JDT(S)$.
3:     $A \leftarrow$ variables in critical annotation.
4:     $MissingVariables \leftarrow S \setminus A$.
5:     **if** $MissingVariables$ empty **then**
6:         return S.
7:     $X_k \leftarrow$ first variable in $MissingVariables$ in lexicographical order.
8:     $B_k \leftarrow$ one of the branches containing X_k in its annotation and has minimum difference to the critical branch.
9:     $S \leftarrow S+$ variables which make difference between B_k and the critical branch.
10: **until** $MissingVariables$ is empty.

---

one level, the search for an MDS set is continued further for the alternative that contains the maximum number of variables from the set S in the critical annotation.

Algorithm 5: Heuristic2 (with heuristic search for choosing minimum difference branches and backtracking on these alternatives)

Input: $\{\{S\}, \{X_i\}, I = \{v_1, v_2\}\}$

1: Construct $JDT(S)$.
2: $A \leftarrow$ variables in critical annotation.
3: $MissingVariables \leftarrow S \setminus A$.
4: **if** $MissingVariables$ empty **then**
5:     return S.
6: $X_k \leftarrow$ first variable from $MissingVariables$ in lexicographical order.
7: $MinimumBranches \leftarrow$ all JDT branches with minimum variables difference to critical branch.
8: **repeat**
9:     $S \leftarrow S+$ variables making difference between critical branch and branch B_k take in their found order from $MinimumBranches$.
10:     $MDS \leftarrow$ Algorithm 5 : Procedure Search–$MDS(S, X_i, I)$.
11: **until** MDS not null or B_k last branch for the set $MinimumBranches$.
12: **if** MDS not found **then**
13:     $S \leftarrow$ the annotation A found in previous $JDTs$ which contains maximum number of variables from S.
14:     $MDS \leftarrow$ Procedure Search–$MDS(S)$.

For a complete algorithm one should search all the alternative branches and not only the ones with minimum distance to the critical branch. Also the search should be continued not only for the annotation with maximum variables from the input set S. But this algorithm tends to be too complex and thus, less efficient.

As shown in our experimental evaluation discussed below, we get a good occurrence of an MDS set with heuristic based search.

Complexity of MDS Algorithm

The computation of the minimal dependent set based on Algorithm 3 for an input of one critical variable X_i and an interchange begins with the computation of the discrimination tree for the two values to interchange which has a time complexity $O(n \cdot d)$, where n represents the number of variables in the CSP [8], and d is the maximum domain size. [9] The time complexity for determining the differences between the branches is $O((n-1) \cdot d \cdot log((n-1) \cdot d))$, thus $O(n \cdot d \cdot log(n \cdot d))$. The space complexity for storing the tree is $O(n \cdot d)$.

If the values are not NI, the search continues as in Algorithm 3, step 6 with Algorithm 4 for the set S containing the critical variable and the variables which make differences between the branches. The construction of the JDT for S, has time complexity $O(s \cdot (n-s) \cdot d^2)$, where s represents the size of the set S, n the size of the CSP and d the maximal domain size, see Chouciry and Noubir [28]. If the set found by this JDT computation is not a minimal dependent set, the search continues with selecting the branch containing values for the missing variable in MDS. The complexity for choosing a branch and comparing with the critical one is $O(d \cdot O(Compare - Branches))$, where $O(Compare - Branches) = O((n-s-1) \cdot d \cdot log((n-s-1) \cdot d))$. The highest time complexity grow is though for computing the JDT of the set S. The overall complexity is therefore $O(s \cdot (n-s) \cdot d^2)$ and thus the time complexity bound stays $O(n^2 \cdot d^2)$ as in JDT construction.

The space complexity is bounded by the space complexity for constructing the JDT which is $O((n-s) \cdot d^2)$.

When the search is done based on $Heuristic2$ as in Algorithm 5, the time complexity increases to $O(n^2 \cdot d^3)$. Also, the space complexity increases to $O((n-s) \cdot d^2)$ as we have to store all the JDT structures computed for all alternative branches having minimum distance to the critical branch.

We can show that:

Theorem 2.2: Multiple MDS.
For a given input set, there might exist more then one MDS set.

Proof. Suppose, we have a set $S = \{X_i, X_1\}$, where X_i represents the critical variable and let I be its set of values to be interchanged. We construct the JDT for

---

[8]In the worse case the critical variable X_i is connected to all the variables in the CSP.

[9]In the case that the input is a set of variables with their interchange sets the complexity grows to $O(s \cdot (n-s) \cdot d^2)$, where s is the size of the input set S, n is the size of the CSP and d is the maximum domain size.

set S where any value of X_1 does not reach the critical annotation. Suppose there are two alternatives (branches) for continuing the search which have a minimum difference to the critical branch: one for a variable X_2 and the other for X_3. By proceeding further search for set $S_1 = \{X_i, X_1, X_2\}$ and $S_2 = \{X_i, X_1, X_3\}$ respectively, we might find that the critical annotations of $JDT(S_1)$ and $JDT(S_2)$ respectively, contain values for all variables in S_1 and S_2 respectively, and thus MDS sets, with possible different domain partitions for variables in S_1 or S_2 for all the variables except the critical one X_i. □

Theorem 2.3: Termination.
Algorithm 3 for computing MDS set terminates.

Proof. The algorithm grows the dependent set incrementally and reconstructs each time its JDT. When the critical annotation contains an MDS set which satisfy all the characteristics, see MDS set characteristics in Section 2.5.1, than it contains an MDS set and the algorithm returns it.

In the worst case, all the CSP variables will be included in the dependent set and the algorithm terminates [10]. □

Theorem 2.4: Soundness.
Algorithm 3 is sound: if it returns an MDS set S, then the set S is a minimal one.

Proof. In the Algorithm 3, we include in the dependent set S the variables making the difference between the branches having in their annotations values to interchange from I.

In the JDT of the new constructed S, the values to interchange of the critical variable will reach the same annotation, the critical one. The algorithm returns the MDS set found in the critical annotation. Thus, the MDS set returned satisfy the first characteristic of a MDS set, see MDS set characteristics in Section 2.5.1.

The algorithm returns only when the NPI set of the $JDT(S)$ contains values for all the variables in the dependent set S. This satisfies the second characteristic in order to be a MDSset.

As proven in 2.5.1, the critical branch of a $JDT(S)$ contains always values for all the neighbor variables of S, so the third characteristic of a MDS set is satisfied.

As in the Algorithm 3, the set S is enlarged incrementally based on neighborhood relations, all the variables in the dependent set S are connected, fact which satisfies the fourth characteristic of a MDS set.

We can conclude that the Algorithm 3 is sound. □

---

[10]This happens in the case when the CSP is connected; otherwise, the algorithm worst case terminates when all the variables connected to the critical variable are included in the dependent set

Theorem 2.5: Completeness.
MDS algorithm is complete in finding one of the MDS sets.

Proof. Algorithm 3 is complete in the sense that it will always return one of the minimal dependent sets. In the worst case the dependent set might spread to the entire CSP. As proven in Theorem 2.3 the algorithm terminates and returns an MDS set which is sound according to Theorem 2.4.   □

Applying MDS – An Example

In the following, we show how NI and MDS algorithms can be applied for solution adaptation on a simple example.

The example in Figure 2.5 represents a CSP where the constraints are binary and denotes mutual exclusion with respect to the values.

It is inspired from Choueiry and Noubir [28].

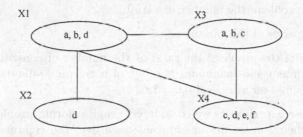

Figure 2.5: CSP example with mutual constraints.

A change on one variable may necessitate changes in other variables in order to stay solution. We apply the MDS algorithm described before in order to calculate minimal set of variables to which the change is localized.

By applying the MDS algorithm on the simple example in the Figure 2.5, we obtain the following results:

From X_1	MDS:	$X_1 = \{a, b\}$	From X_2	–	
found:		$X_3 = \{a, b\}$	found:		
From X_3	MDS:	$X_1 = \{a, b\}$	From X_4	NI:	$X_4 = \{e, f\}$
found:		$X_3 = \{a, b\}$	found:	MDS:	$X_3 = \{c\}$
	MDS:	$X_3 = \{c\}$			$X_4 = \{c, e, f\}$
		$X_4 = \{c, e, f\}$		MDS:	$X_4 = \{c, d, e, f\}$
	MDS:	$X_3 = \{a, c\}$			$X_1 = \{a, b\}$
		$X_1 = \{a, b\}$			$X_3 = \{a, b, c\}$
		$X_4 = \{c, d, e, f\}$			

NI appears in very sparse $CSPs$ with density less then 0.4. In the following we study how the occurrence of the MDS sets depends on the CSP problem structure.

Experimental results

The performance of the algorithm for finding MDS sets depends on the structure of the CSP problem.

In the following, we present the results we obtained on empirical tests for studying this dependence.

Experimental Model

The following results are from tests analyzing the number and *spread* (size) of MDS sets detected w.r.t. varying *CSP configuration* (structure). The CSP parameters we consider in our experiments are:

1. size of the problem: the number of variables.

2. the domain sizes of the variables.

3. the *density* of the problem: the ratio of the number of constraints relatively to the minimum and maximum number of constraints allowed in the given CSP, measured on a scale of $0.0 - 1.0$.

During these experiments we considered graph coloring problems randomly generated. As their constraints are mutual exclusive, the tightness of the constraints, which represents the fraction of the combinatorially possible pairs that are allowed by the constraint between two variables, is not taken into consideration.

Following the model of measuring the NI set as in [25], we report the results only for problem sizes $n = 10$ and $n = 20$, while varying the density (dens–csp) in $\{0.1, 0.2, \ldots, 1\}$ of the CSP and the maximum domain size dom–size = $\{\frac{n}{10}, \frac{2n}{10}, \ldots, \frac{9n}{10}, n\}$. For each case, we generate random problems and then graphically represented by considering the measures described below.

Let us consider the CSP problem $G = (V, E)$ as a constraint graph where V represents the vertices (variables) and E edges (constraints), and

- nMDS(X_i) – represents the number of value pairs of variable $X_i \in V$ for which there is an MDS.

- avMDS(X_i) $= \frac{\sum_{k=1}^{nMDS} size(k)}{nMDS}$ is the average size of an MDS set for variable $X_i \in V$, where size(k) represents the number of variables in the current MDS set, where by the size of an MDS set we understand the number of variables in the MDS set.

- $\|V\|$ is the number of variables that has at least one pair of values that spread in a MDS set over their entire domain (all possible pair values).

In our test evaluation we compute the density of the problem as: dens–csp $= \frac{e-e\_min}{e\_max-e\_min}$, where e represents the number of edges in the current CSP, e_min $= n - 1$ and $e\_max = \frac{n(n-1)}{2}$, where n is the size of the problem CSP.

Results

We now introduce the three criteria we used to measure the existence and spread of MDS sets in the CSP.

Spread: of the MDS sets. m1 measures the 'spread' of the minimal dependent sets (MDS sets) in the sense that we computed the average size of the MDS set in a given CSP:

$$m1 = \frac{\sum_{k=1}^{\|V\|} avMDS(Vk)}{\|V\|}$$

We have the graphical representation of $m1$ measure in Figure 2.6 for problems of size 10 and in Figure 2.7 for problems of size 20. We can see that for problems with low density the spread tends to 0. As expected this means that in low density problems exchanging the values of one variable does not propagate too much in the CSP (corresponds to NI). This indicates that NI adaptation could be successfully applied here. When the density of the CSP increases, the size, spread, of MDS sets, tends to increase as well. Moreover, spread increases with the number of resources. The two metrics applied to measuring the number of MDS occurrences, as defined in [25], are as follows:

Occurrence 1: existence of the MDS sets. m2 measures the 'occurrence' of MDS sets in a given CSP in the sense that it computes how many variables generate MDS sets in association with the size of the problem.

$$m2 = \frac{\|V\|}{n}$$

Looking at Figures 2.8 and 2.9 we have the proof that MDS occurs often in any CSP configuration and increases with the density of the CSP as well as with the number of resources.

Occurrence 2: existence of the MDS sets. m3 measures the 'occurrence' of MDS sets in the sense that it computes the average number of MDS sets per variable.

$$m3 = \frac{\sum_{k=1}^{\|V\|} nMDS(Xk)}{n}$$

The average number of MDS sets per variable depends in the same way as Occurrence 1 on the configuration of the CSP, but it is a better indicator w.r.t the density of the problem and highly dependent on the number of resources, see Figure 2.10 and Figure 2.11.

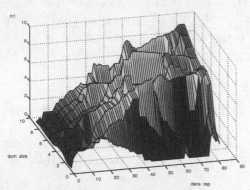

Figure 2.6: Spread of *MDS* sets for random generated *CSPs* with size 10.

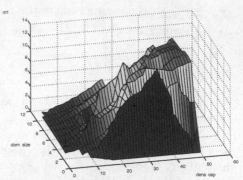

Figure 2.7: Spread of *MDS* sets for random generated *CSP* with size 20.

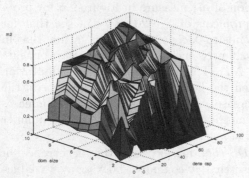

Figure 2.8: Occurrence of *MDS* sets per variable in random *CSPs* with size 10.

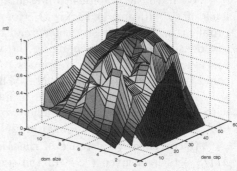

Figure 2.9: Occurrence of *MDS* sets per variable in random *CSPs* with size 20.

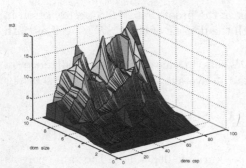

Figure 2.10: Average number of *MDS* sets per variable in random *CSPs* with size 10.

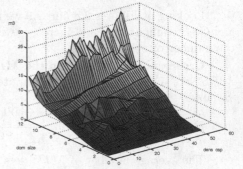

Figure 2.11: Average number of *MDS* sets per variable in random *CSPs* with size 20.

From the results we can conclude that on higher density problems the occurrence of PI characterized through MDS sets, increases and thus, the range of the adaptation increases as well with it, but in the same time the spread is enlarged over the variables of the CSP. When the spread enlarges, the effect of a change propagates further. Thus at a certain point, searching the MDS sets should be stopped. When the MDS set becomes too large, it might not bring any additional profit, as it would be equivalent to or even more costly than solving the problem from scratch.

Some conclusions

Until now, interchangeability has mostly been applied as a technique for enhancing search and backtracking, see [43] and [48]. It had not been effectively exploited as a technique for updating solutions. In this work we have studied how interchangeability can be applied for updating solutions with the goal of using it further in solution adaptation. The work makes the following main contributions:

- A complete algorithm for detecting MDS sets which can be used to provide more flexible adaptation than an NI only based approach would.

- An evaluation of how far changes propagate in solutions to be adapted according to problem structure (investigating impact of density and size of the problem), indicating:

  - Strong dependency on the density parameter of the CSP where MDS are more frequent in $CSPs$ with high density.

  - Weak dependency on the domain sizes where MDS increases also with the number of resources.

2.5.2   Minimum Dependent Set Algorithm (mDS)

We study now algorithms for computing minimum dependent sets of interchangeable values in $CSPs$.

In general, changes to an existing solution are hard to implement, so it is required to find the minimum dependent set among the minimal ones.

Description of the algorithm

We show in the following how to compute the minimum set of variables and their corresponding values to which the change is localized when interchanging a values pair of a CSP variable. We called this set *the minimum dependent set (mDS)*.

There are many ways in which an interchange of pair of values for one variable can propagate through a CSP, thus there are many minimal dependent sets but fewer minimum ones.

In the Section 2.5.1, we described an algorithm for computing a minimal dependent set. The search is based on the JDT structure and for computing the

MDS sets we use heuristics for choosing further search alternative branch which contains in its annotation variables/values we need to include in the dependent set. This heuristic approach helps for reducing the algorithm complexity.

Computing the minimum set among all the minimal ones requires optimality as we have to compute all the possible minimal and then choose the minimum among all of them. This optimality condition increases the algorithm complexity. We attempt to reduce the complexity by considering as search limit the neighboring degrees of variables to the critical variable, called K-*distance*.

The algorithm for finding the mDS set for a given interchangeable set of a CSP variable X_i proceeds in the same way as the MDS algorithm except that when a variable is missing from the critical annotation we have to consider further search for all branches containing the missing variable in the annotation. Further the search continues in a branch and bound way in the sense that we do not continue the search for MDS sets containing more variables then the minimum one found so far.

In the following we give the main steps of the mDS algorithm. In the first 3 steps, the algorithm is similar to the MDS one.

1. Start by constructing the DT for the variable X_i and its values in the interchange set $I = \{v_1, v_2\}$.

2. If the values v_1 and v_2 are not in the annotation of the same branch, reconstruct the JDT of a set formed by the variable X_i and the variables found to make a difference in the branches for the values to interchange.

3. If the actual JDT contains in its critical annotation a minimal dependent set then this is the minimum one and the search is stopped.

4. If this is not the case, we proceed further search for sets candidates by comparing the critical branch with all the branches containing in their annotations values of the first variable V_k which is missing from the critical annotation. The new candidate sets are obtained by adding the variables making the difference between the critical branch and the chosen branch to the set for which the current JDT was constructed. For each candidate set, the corresponding JDT is constructed and thus, either some new MDS sets are found or the search continues with new candidate sets.

5. During the computation the minimum MDS set found is memorized and the search is not continued for candidate set alternatives that are larger than the last minimum found. We consider all the alternatives for further search, thus the algorithm is optimal.

6. The algorithm terminates either when a neighboring K–distance from the critical variable X_i is reached (no sense to search further, the dependent set would be too big) or when we have a MDS set MDS_i which is the minimum among all the MDS found by now and all the other further search sets

candidates are larger then the set which gave MDS_i. Then MDS_i is the minimum dependent set mDS.

The mDS algorithm is given below, see Algorithm 6:

Algorithm 6: Algorithm for Searching a Minimum Dependent Set (mDS) in a K–distance neighboring,
(Input: X_i, $I = \{v_0, v_1\}$)

1:   $S \leftarrow \{X_i\}$.
2:   Construct the $DT(X_i)$ for values in I.
3:   **if** v_1 and v_2 in different annotations **then**
4:      $S \leftarrow$ insert variables which make the differences between the branches having in their annotations v_1 and v_2.
5:      $CandidateSets \leftarrow \{S\}$
6:      **repeat**
7:         **for** Each $S' \in CandidateSets$ **do**
8:             Construct $JDT(S')$.
9:             $Candidates_{mDS} \leftarrow$ insert critical annotation of $JDT(S')$
10:            $MainCandidate \leftarrow$ the minimum size $Candidate_{mDS}$ among all the $Candidates_{mDS}$.
11:            **for** Each $Candidate_{mDS} \in Candidates_{mDS}$ with size smaller then $MainCandidate$ (if there is no $MainCandidate$ yet continue with all the candidates). **do**
12:               Continue search though all the branches containing in their annotations the first variable V_k in the lexicographical order which is missing from the $Candidate_{mDS}$.
13:               Compute new candidate sets, where the candidate sets are computed by adding the variables making difference between the critical branch and the chosen branch to the candidate set for which the current JDT was constructed.
14:               $CandidateSets \leftarrow$ insert the new candidate set which are smaller then $MainCandidate$.
15:      **until** K–distance is reached or $CandidateSets == 0$
16: **else**
17:      $mDS \leftarrow \{X_i\}$ (the values v_1, v_2 are NI).
18: **return** mDS for variable X_i and values in I.

The minimum dependent set algorithm can be also extended in a straightforward manner. In the same way as MDS algorithm, for an input containing a set of critical variables with their corresponding interchange values sets. [11] The idea remains the same: we try to bring in the annotation of the same branch all

---

[11] The generalization to a set critical variables is straightforward and obtained by starting the algorithm from step 2.

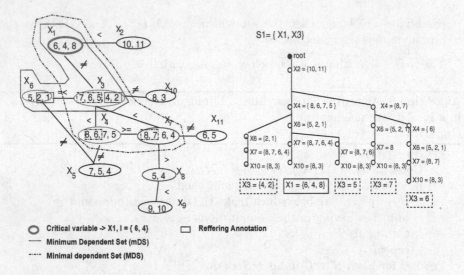

Figure 2.12: CSP example. We want to calculate minimum dependent set (mDS) for variable X_1 and the interchange set $I = \{6, 4\}$.

the variables from the input with the corresponding value–pairs by including the set the variables which make the difference between the branches.

In the following we give an example of applying the minimum dependent set algorithm on the CSP problem in Figure 2.12, left side. For example, we consider the critical variable X_1 and the interchange set $I = \{6, 4\}$. The DT of X_1 is constructed for the values in the interchange I. These values do not reach the same branch annotation. Thus, the values in I are not NI and by interchanging them the change will spread to other variables. We proceed further search in order to find the minimum set of variables to which the change spreads. As variable X_3 is making the difference between the branches we form the set $S_1 = \{X_1, X_3\}$ and reconstruct the JDT for it, see Figure 2.12, the right side.

The JDT for set S_1 finds in the critical annotation [12] only values for variable X_1, but any value for the variable X_3. If the mDS algorithm searches for a 1–distance mDS set, the algorithm stops here without finding any mDS set. For any K higher then 1 the algorithm continues in the following way:

The search is continued by considering all the branches having in their annotations values for X_3 which is the missing variable in the critical annotation, see Figure 2.12. The search is continued, first for branches which have minimum number of variables relative to the critical branch. So, in our example for the branch with annotation $X_3 = \{4, 2\}$, the difference to the critical branch is variable X_6, and for the branch with the annotation $X_3 = \{5\}$, the difference to the critical

---

[12]We remind that the critical annotation is the one which contains the critical variable X_1 and the values to interchange from set I.

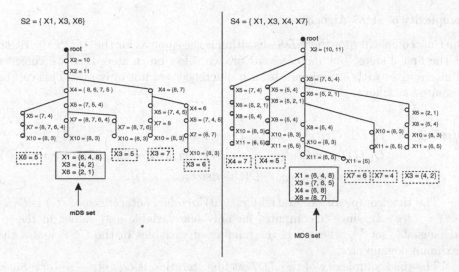

Figure 2.13: The minimum dependent set (mDS) and the minimal dependent set (MDS) for variable X_1 and the interchange set $I = \{6, 4\}$ in Figure 2.12.

branch is variable X_7. For the other two branches the difference to the critical branch is higher as they differ for variables X_4 and X_7 as well.

By constructing the JDT for set $S_2 = \{X_1, X_3, X_6\}$ we find an mDS set with domain partitions as in Figure 2.13, left side.

The JDT for set $S_3 = \{X_1, X_3, X_7\}$, is missing values for variable X_7 in the critical annotation and further searching must proceed by reiterating the operation on branches as before. Anyway, as inserting at least one variable in set S_3 gives a bigger set size than S_2, the mDS algorithm stops and returns the mDS found for set S_2.

In the MDS algorithm, we select the branch with minimum variables difference between branches as the heuristic. In the example of Figure 2.12, we find two branches having a difference of only one variable as mentioned before: one which differs by X_6 and the other by X_7. If the branch having the difference X_7 is chosen instead of the one with the difference X_6, which leads to the minimum dependent set, we continue the iteration for set S_3 which does not contain an MDS set in the critical node. Using the same heuristic, by constructing the JDT for set S_3, we find a branch which differs with only variable X_4.

The JDT structure for set $S_4 = \{X_1, X_3, X_4, X_7\}$ finds an MDS set as in the Figure 2.13, on the right.

So, the minimum dependent set for critical variable X_1 and values to interchange $I = \{6, 4\}$ is as in the Figure 2.13, on the left : $X_1 = \{6, 4, 8\}, X_3 = \{4, 2\}, X_6 = \{2, 1\}$, at a 2–distance from the critical variable.

Complexity of mDS Algorithm

The time complexity for the mDS algorithm is the same as for the MDS algorithm for the first 3 steps, but increases for branch selection in step 4, as we consider all alternatives with a minimum branch difference and not only one. This can be computed as follows:

$$
\begin{aligned}
O(mDS & = & O(DT(Critical_{Variable}, Interchange_{Set})) \\
& + & O(JDT(Critical_{Variable} + DifferenceVariablesinDTbranches)) \\
& + & O(Branches_{Number} \cdot O(Compare_{Branches}))
\end{aligned}
$$

The time complexity of $O(DT(CriticalVariable, InterchangeSet))$ is $O(n \cdot 2 \cdot d) = O(n \cdot d)$, since it computes for only one variable and values in the interchangeable set [13], where n is the number of variables in the CSP and d the maximum domain size.

The time complexity of the JDT at first iteration is $O(s \cdot (n - s) \cdot d^2)$. Since in the worst case we would obtain d alternatives, branches, the time complexity grows to $O(s \cdot (n - s) \cdot d^3)$, where s is the size of the dependent set S, n is the size of the CSP and d the domain size. As s grows to n, the time complexity becomes $O(n^2 \cdot d^3)$.

The time complexity for choosing branches and comparing them remains as in the MDS algorithm: $O(d \cdot O((n - s) \cdot d \cdot log((n - s) \cdot d)))$.

Since the complexity for computing the $JDTs$ is the highest, the overall time complexity for the mDS algorithm is $O(n^2 \cdot d^3)$.

The space complexity is given by the space needed to store the JDT structures at each iteration. As we can compute one by one the JDT structures, the space complexity remains as that needed for storing one JDT at a time: $O((n - s) \cdot d)$.

To reduce complexity we imposed the K–distance parameter which limits the search to a K neighboring distance from the critical variable. This method is useful for sparse problems with a density smaller than 0.5, while for very dense problems it is not effective. In very dense problems the complexity of mDS algorithm might increase so much that it might be more effective to search only a minimal dependent set based on branch heuristic search, as in Section 2.5.1.

We can show that:

Theorem 2.6

mDS algorithm terminates.

mDS algorithm is sound: if it returns a mDS set S, then the set S is a minimum one.

mDS algorithm is complete: if there exists a mDS set it will find it.

---

[13] In the case that the interchangeable set reaches the domain size the time complexity grows to $O(n \cdot d^2)$

Proof. Termination:

Algorithm 6 searches in a branch and bound manner for the minimum dependent set among the minimal ones. When a minimal dependent set S is found, the alternatives which might increase the size of the dependent set more then the size of S are dropped down. So, in the case where the algorithm finds MDS sets, it selects the minimum one and drops all the search paths which increase the dependent set more then the last minimum one found. When all the search alternatives are reaching K–distance from the critical variable, Algorithm 6 stops and returns the minimum dependent set. As in Algorithm 3, in the worst case, the algorithm can continue until the entire CSP is covered if no MDS set is found by then, or the K–distance is sufficiently large [14]. When no MDS set is found up to a K–distance, the Algorithm 6 stops and returns null.

Soundness:

Algorithm 6 is sound when we do not impose the K–distance condition. Algorithm 6 computes the minimum dependent set among the minimal ones. Suppose we find a 2–distance MDS_2 set, which has a size k, and also an alternative branch which has an incomplete annotation $ANNOT$, where not all variables from S reach the annotation. As the size of $ANNOT$ smaller then MDS_2, for the 3–distance search continues for this branch, suppose we find and MDS_3 set with a size smaller than MDS_2, such that it becomes the minimum one. If the algorithm stops at 2 distance, it would not in fact find the minimum one. To find the mDS, one has to consider all alternatives.

Completeness:

Algorithm 6 is complete only when we do not impose the K–distance heuristic. Without this condition, the algorithm searches until it finds a minimal dependent set MDS, do not follow the search alternatives which would increase the size of the dependent set more than MDS. In this way it selects the minimum among all the MDS sets found. In the worse case the algorithm has to search all the alternatives and the dependent set might spread to the entire CSP. □

Experimental results

The performance of the algorithm for finding minimum dependent sets depends very much on the structure of the CSP problem. The following results are from random tests and they analyze the existence, in number, and the size of minimum dependent sets detected w.r.t. varying CSP configuration structure.

A constraint satisfaction problem can mainly be characterized by the following 4 parameters:

- n – the number of variables,

- a – the maximum domain size,

---

[14]Note that in very dense problem K–distance limitation does not help to reduce the complexity.

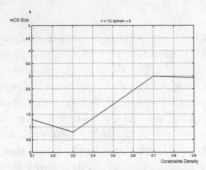

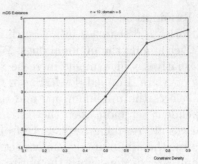

Figure 2.14: Average Size of mDS sets in random generated CSPs with size 10.

Figure 2.15: Average number of mDS sets per variable in random generated CSPs with size 10, obtained by interchanging all the values from the variable domain.

- d – the constraint density of the CSP problem: the ratio of the number of constraints relatively to the minimum and maximum number of the constraints allowed in the given CSP, measured on a scale $0.0 - 1.0$,

- t – the tightness of the constraints: the fraction of the number of forbidden tuples to the number of all possible tuples.

In our measurement we have considered only the first 3 parameters thus far. We run the minimum dependent set algorithm on randomly generated $CSPs$. The tests are restricted to binary $CSPs$.

In the following we describe the criteria we used to measure the existence and size of minimum dependent

Size: The mDS–Size is the average size (the number of variables) of a minimum dependent set (mDS).

$$mDS - Size = \frac{\sum_{k=1}^{\|V_{mDS}\|} \frac{\sum_{j=1}^{mDS_{Sets}(X_k)} \|S_j(Xk)\|}{\|mDS_{Sets}(X_k)\|}}{\|V_{mDS}\|},$$

where V_{mDS} is the set of variables which have mDS sets obtained by interchanging all the values from their domain, $mDS_{Sets}(X_k)$ represents all mDS sets of variable X_k.

It has been shown that the neighborhood interchangeability (NI) appears for a density lower then 0.4, see [5], [25].

It has been proved that there is less neighborhood partial interchangeability characterized by MDS sets for low density, but it occurs as the density increases, see [69]. mDS sets are computed by counting NI and MDS sets occurrence. For $CSPs$ with low density mDS sets tend to be small and sometimes have an average of only one variable with its NI values where as for high density $CSPs$ mDS increases in size to more variables and their values to interchange values.

In Figure 2.14, we show how the average size of mDS varies depending on the constraint density of the CSP for problems of size $n = 10$ and maximum domain size $a = 10$. Each point on the graph was obtained by computing the average over 50 random generated problems. Our experiments prove that the size of mDS sets increase with the constraint density and have manageable sizes.

Existence: The Existence measures the 'existence' of minimum dependent sets (mDS) sets in the sense that it computes the average number of mDS sets per variable.

$$mDS - Existence = \frac{\sum_{k=1}^{\|V_{mDS}\|} \|mDS_{Sets}(X_k)\|}{n},$$

where V_{mDS} is the set of variables which have mDS sets obtained by interchanging all the values from its domain, $\|mDS_{Sets}(X_k)\|$ is the number of mDS sets of variable X_k.

In Figure 2.15, we have the graphical representation of the mDS–Existence. It can be observed that the existence of MDS sets increases with the CSP density.

Some conclusions

Our main contribution is the algorithm for searching minimum dependent sets by localized search based on the interchangeability concept. The algorithm results can be used to find close solutions by minimum changes to already known solutions. This algorithm can provide the basic for classifying the CSP solutions method and for constructing families of solutions.

By applying this algorithm to randomly generated problems, we have gained an understanding of the existence and size of minimum dependent sets depending on domain sizes and constraint density.

Briefly the main conclusions are:

- Strong dependency on the density parameter of the CSP where mDS sets are more frequent in $CSPs$ with high density.

- Weak dependency on the domains sizes where mDS size increases with the number of resources.

The results show that mDS sets of manageable size exist for all variables/values and that they can be computed with a manageable amount of effort. This makes partial interchangeability an interesting concept for practical applications.

2.6 Partial Interchangeability – Tuple Interchangeability

Today, algorithms for computing partial interchangeability, as neighborhood partial interchangeability in [28] and those proposed in Section 2.5.1 and Section 2.5.2, localize the change to a set S of CSP variables, but the consistencies among the variables inside this set S are not guaranteed.

In the following, we propose algorithms that compute partial interchangeable solutions, which we call *interchangeable tuples*. These tuples correspond to consistent value assignments inside set S, which satisfy in the same way the neighboring and thus, the rest of the CSP.

2.6.1 Introduction and Definitions

There are no known polynomial algorithms to compute partial interchangeability, as in Definition 2.4. Computing the partial interchangeable sets amounts, in general, to the enumeration of all solutions to the CSP, which is far too expensive.

As shown in the Section 2.5.1, a localized algorithm for computing partial interchangeable sets was proposed by Choueiry and Noubir under the name *neighborhood partial interchangeability (NPI)*.

As we show further in this section NPI does not always implies PI. In previous Section 2.5.1, we proposed algorithms to compute minimal/minimum set of variables to which the change is spread for a given pair of values to interchange. Again this algorithms are localizing the change to a set of CSP variables and determine their value domain partitions which allow interchange of values inside these partitions without affecting the neighborhood and thus, the rest of the CSP. However, all these algorithms arrive to localize the change to a set of variables and their domain partitions with no guarantee that there exist valid assignments for variables inside these sets.

In the following, our purpose is to study algorithms that search for interchangeable consistent assignments, partial solutions of the CSP, which we called *tuple interchangeability*. As the algorithms we propose are also based on localized and neighborhood relations in the CSP, we call this method *neighborhood tuple interchangeability (NTI)*. These tuples are computed as consistent assignments to the dependent set obtained by the spread of change for a certain interchange, i.e. the interchange of a pair of values for a CSP variable [15].

So, we propose a new concept called *neighborhood tuple interchangeability (NTI)* which can approximate PI properly. The scenario for the algorithm which generates approximated PI sets follows two steps: (1) use NPI as a filter for the

---

[15]The algorithms we give, for minimal/minimum dependent set search and for tuple interchangeable search, can be straightforwardly extended for more extensive inputs as a set of variable instead of only one and whose values to be interchanged over a domain partition instead only a pair.

computation of NTI sets , and (2) compute the NTI sets. As NTI implies PI, as we prove further, we find PI sets.

Consider the example in Figure 2.1. By applying the algorithm proposed by Choueiry and Noubir [28], we find that the values w and s for variable X_5 are *neighborhood partial interchangeable* with respect to set $S = \{X_2\}$. At the same time, we can see that the values w and s of variable X_5 also satisfy the Definition 2.4 of partial interchangeability as for one solution where $X_5 = w$ implies a solution with $X_5 = s$ and with possible changes for X_4 in the case this has assigned w or s. A problem associated with this algorithm is that it does not indicate how to choose the set of variables S on which the algorithm is applied.

Partial interchangeability might be hard to compute without enumeration of all solutions. There are partial interchangeable values which are hard to detect by using neighborhood based algorithms. For example, the variable X_3 of the CSP in the Figure 2.1, has value t *partially interchangeable* with value v with respect to the set $S = \{X_2\}$ because the variable X_0 will never take value t in a consistent solution as X_1 always equals t. This form of partial interchangeability is hard to compute in a localized manner and by now, there are no computable algorithms to find these partial interchangeable values.

Moreover, NPI does not necessarily imply PI. For example, by computing NPI values for critical variable X_2, interchangeable set $I = \{x, r\}$, and dependent set $S = \{X_0\}$, we find the following NPI values sets: $X_2 = \{x, r\}, X_0 = \{x\}$. Thus, NPI finds that values x and r for variable X_2 are NPI but they do not fulfill the partial interchangeability Definition 2.4. By interchanging value x for r for variable X_2 there is no solution in this case as variable X_0 can take only value x, not compatible for $X_2 = x$.

We propose here an algorithm which approximates PI and guarantees that the values found are PI.

As it appears in Definition 2.5, NPI localizes variables values without guarantee of consistency among the values inside the NPI set.

The definition we propose further describes consistent partial consistent tuples/solutions which satisfy the neighborhood in the same way:

Definition 2.9 (Neighborhood Tuple Interchangeability – NTI) Values $X_i = a$ and $X_i = b$ are *tuple* interchangeable (NTI) with respect to a set of variables S if for every *consistent* tuple t of value assignments to $S \cup \{X_i\}$ that admits $X_i = a$ there is another *consistent* tuple t' that admits $X_i = b$ such that t and t' are consistent with the same value combinations for variables outside of S. Additionally, the same condition must hold with a and b exchanged.

In this work, we propose an algorithm which computes *neighborhood tuple interchangeable (NTI)* values and thus approximates PI. In the Figure 2.1, for the critical variable X_3 and interchangeable set $I = \{t, z, q\}$ our NTI algorithm finds as dependent set the set of variables $S = \{X_2, X_0\}$ and all its consistent tuples, as in Table 2.1.

Theorem 2.7

(Extensivity: $NTI \implies NPI$) Consider a critical variable X_i. If values a and b are NTI with dependent set S, then they are NPI with dependent set S.

Proof. By Definition 2.9, if values a and b of variable X_i are NTI with respect to the dependent set S, for every consistent tuple t_a of value assignments to $S \cup \{X_i\}$ where $X_i = a$, there exists a consistent tuple tuple t_b that admits $X_i = b$. t_a and t_b are consistent with the neighborhood of $S \cup \{X_i\}$. Then, if the set of variables S is removed from the problem, values a and b are both consistent with the neighborhood in the same way, thus NI with the problem. This makes them NPI according to the Definition 2.5. $\qquad\square$

Theorem 2.8

(Extensivity: $NTI \implies PI$) Consider a critical variable X_i. If values a and b are NTI with dependent set S, then they are PI with dependent set S.

Proof. By Definition 2.9, if tuples t_a and t_b are NTI, they are compatible in the same way with the neighborhood of the dependent set S. Thus, by replacing t_a with t_b in a given solution, it will stay a solution. So, for a solution which contains a there is another solution which contains b with changes only in set S. By Definition 2.4, this means that values a and b in the interchangeable set I are PI. $\qquad\square$

Theorem 2.9

Let I be a partially interchangeable set for critical variable X_i with dependent set S. Then I is also a neighborhood tuple interchangeable set for X_i with dependent set $S' \supseteq S$.

Proof. If I is PI then there is a set of solutions to the entire problem that contain all values in I. These solutions make I NTI with respect to a set S' which contains all variables of the problem. $\qquad\square$

Of course, in most cases, it will not be necessary to extend the dependent set to the entire problem to obtain NTI. Theorem 2.9 is useful since it allows us to prove that a set I is not PI whenever we can show that it cannot be NTI.

For example, in the problem from Figure 2.1 the set $I = \{t, v\}$ is *partially interchangeable* for the variable X_3 with the dependent set $S = \{X_0\}$. This happens because variable X_0 would never take value t but this is not computationally tractable. By using NTI, we can find that I is a *neighborhood tuple interchangeable* set for X_3 with dependent set $S' = \{X_0, X_2\}$, where $S' \supseteq S$.

2.6.2   Algorithm for Computing Neighborhood Tuple Interchangeability (NTI)

Our main objective is to find equivalent tuples of values, partial CSP solutions, which satisfy in the same way the rest of the problem relative to its neighborhood.

According to this property, they can be interchanged in a given solution without affecting the rest of the problem.

We therefore propose a more refined search algorithm than MDS algorithms, see Section 2.5.1, which computes consistency inside the set of variables S to which the change is localized the change and guides the search according to them as well.

The algorithm is based also on the discrimination tree structure defined by Freuder [41] at some stages of search, and the Joint Discrimination Tree (JDT) algorithm by Choueiry et al., [28]. See Section 2.2 for these algorithms.

Since we are interested in localizing the change in variables of the dependent set S for the interchangeable set I of the critical variable, we limit our search to a neighborhood of S, consistent with the values in the interchangeable set.

So, in the search for tuple interchangeability [16] we need to consider only a part of the JDT, respectively only sub–branches of the branch which contains the interchangeable set of the critical variable/dependent set in its leaf annotation. We define this limited JDT as follows:

Definition 2.10 (Reduced JDT) A *reduced JDT* is a JDT where we consider only the assignments that are compatible with all values in the interchangeable set [17]. We call these assignments the *Common Assignments*.

According to the Definition 2.10, as in the branches of the reduced JDT we consider only assignments of the neighborhood compatible with the interchangeable set, the assignments for all the other variables of the dependent set can be only subsets of the *common assignments*. This property is important in further design of the NTI algorithm.

In Figure 2.16, we represent the discrimination tree for critical variable X_3 of the problem given in the example from Figure 2.1 and its interchangeable set $I = \{t, v\}$. In this example, the *assignments* of the branch which leads to $X_3 = \{t\}$ are the following variable/value combinations: $X_0 = x, X_0 = y, X_0 = v, X_2 = x, X_2 = y, X_2 = z, X_4 = y, X_4 = w$.

In this DT computation, we obtain two *annotations*, one contains value $X_3 = v$ and the other $X_3 = t$. As the values v and t do not end up in the same annotation they are not NI and further search for their tuple interchangeability is necessary.

An example of the reduced JDT for variable X_3, the interchangeable set $I = \{t, v\}$ and the set of variables $S = \{X_0\}$ is given in the left side of Figure 2.17. As in this tree the variable X_0 no longer discriminates the values v and t for variable X_3; these values now belong to the same annotation. They are compatible with the assignments of their own branch and as all the other branches are subsets of their branch, they are compatible with all the assignments in the reduced JDT.

---

[16]These tuples contain values from the interchangeable set I assigned to critical variable and consistent values for the other dependent variables.

[17]In the construction of the reduced JDT for variables from the dependent set S which do not have constraints with direct neighbors of critical variable, thus they are compatible with their entire domain, constructs or move only on the assignments compatible with the values in the interchangeable set.

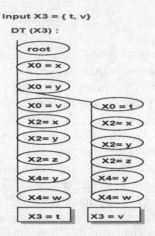

Figure 2.16: Discrimination Tree (DT) of variable X_3 from the problem Figure 2.1.

We now give a description of the algorithm and then present experimental results of tuple interchangeability occurrence relative to the CSP structure.

Algorithm for Construction of Joint Tuple Tree (JTT)

In the following, we introduce a new structure which we call *Joint Tuple Tree (JTT)* used in our algorithm for the computation of interchangeable tuples. The JTT is constructed from the annotations of the reduced JDT and the relations between their corresponding assignments.

By the computation of a JDT for set of variables S, a critical variable X_i and an interchangeable set $I = \{a, b\}$ we obtain various annotations at the leaves of the JDT. The annotations contain values of the variables from the set S compatible with the assignments of the JDT branches.

We define the Joint Tuple Tree which contains the reduced JDT annotations and their relations:

Definition 2.11 (Joint Tuple Tree (JTT)) A *Joint Tuple Tree* is a tree which contains as nodes the leaves of the reduced JDT for a critical variable X_i and a dependent set S. A node n is a child of a node n' if the set of compatible assignments of n is a subset of that of n' and if there is no other n'' such that n'' would be child of n and n' child of n''. We annotate the arc between n and n' by the variables involved in assignments that are consistent with n' but not with n. [18]

For example, for variable X_3 and its interchangeable set $I = \{t, v\}$ in Figure 2.16 we have to continue further search. We can see in Figure 2.16 that variable

---

[18]The JTT arc between its nodes represent subset relations between the node assignments of the reduced JDT branches of the corresponding end nodes annotations.

X_0 is making the difference between branches having in their annotations the values of the interchangeable set. Thus, we further construct the reduced JDT of critical variable X_3, the interchangeable set $I = \{t, v\}$ and the set of variables $S = \{X_0\}$, see Figure 2.17 on the left side. On the right side of the Figure 2.17, we represented the JTT obtained from the annotations of the $JDT(S)$.

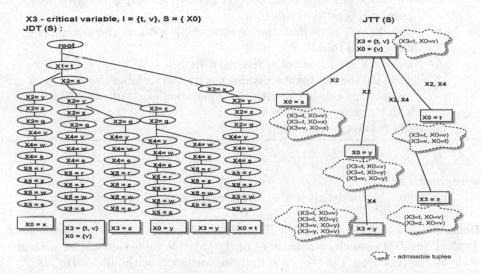

Figure 2.17: Joint Discrimination Tree (JDT) for the critical variable X_3, interchangeable set $I = \{t, v\}$ and dependent set $S = \{X_0\}$ (left side). Joint Tuple Tree (JTT) for the critical variable X_3, interchangeable set $I = \{t, v\}$ and dependent set $S = \{X_0\}$ (right side).

The root node of the JTT contains the critical annotation of the JDT which holds the critical variable X_3 and the interchangeable set $I = \{t, v\}$.

All the other JDT annotations have branch assignments that are subsets of the root node branch assignment, and thus they become children of the root node. As the annotation $X_3 = y$ has the assignments a subset of the annotation X_0, it becomes its child.

In the following we propose an algorithm for constructing the JTT from a reduced JDT. As in Figure 2.17, we consider as root node the leaf of the JDT which contains in its annotation the interchangeable set I of source variable X_i. Further, we adjust the other leaves of the JDT as nodes in the JTT. As in Definition 2.11, a node n is child node of n' when node n contains a subset of its assignments.

Algorithm 7 constructs the tree of dependencies between JDT leaves which are its nodes. It labels the arc between nodes with variables involved in assignments that are consistent with the parent node but not with the child. It labels each node with consistent tuples of dependent set S for which the JDT and respectively JTT

Algorithm 7: Joint Tuple Tree (JTT):

1: $T \leftarrow$ root node, $r =$ leaf node with interchangeable set in reduced JDT.
2: $l \leftarrow$ remaining leaf nodes of the reduced JDT.
3: **repeat**
4:      $n \leftarrow$ node in l such that no other node n' is compatible with all assignments on the path to n.
5:      $p \leftarrow$ deepest node in T that is compatible with all the assignments on the path to n.
6:      make n a child node of p; remove n from l.
7:      annotate the arc between p and n with the variable involved in assignments consistent with the annotation of p but not consistent with the annotation of n.
8: **until** l is empty

---

were constructed.

We define the consistent tuples which label the JTT nodes as follows:

Definition 2.12 (Admissible Tuples) The admissible tuples at a node n of the Joint Tuple Tree (JTT) are all combinations of the variable values associated with any node on the path from the root to n that are consistent with all constraints [19].

Informally, the admissible tuples are all the consistent tuples using assignments in the annotations of the node and its ancestors.

Our interest is to find a node which has admissible tuples containing at least one tuple for each value from the interchangeable set of the critical variable. We define this node as follows:

Definition 2.13 (Compatibility) We call the subtree of the joint tuple tree (JTT) rooted at node n *compatible* if:

- for each value in the interchangeable set, the JTT admissible tuples at node n contain at least one tuple where the critical variable takes that value or

- the admissible tuples at node n contain no tuple where the critical variable takes a value in the interchangeable set, and all subtrees rooted at children of node n are compatible.

Lemma 2.2

A consistent tuple t which is consistent with the neighborhood will be admissible at some node of the JTT.

---

[19] Each JTT is constructed from a JDT of a candidate minimal dependent set S. The variables in nodes are variables of this set S; and in tuple consistency computation associated to JTT nodes, we consider the constraints associated to variables in set S.

Proof. The root node contains values to interchange for the critical variable. All the child nodes contain values for variables in S which are compatible with some subset of the neighborhood of their parents. At each node we compute consistent tuples which contain values from the current node and all the values for variables in S which appear in all the parent nodes on the path to the root node. □

Theorem 2.10
Admissible tuples of a JTT node are interchangeable.

Proof. Let t and t' be two admissible tuples in a JTT node. We prove that if t is compatible is a CSP solution, then t' can replace it and vice versa. Thus, they are interchangeable. Let's suppose that t is part of the solution tuple s of the CSP. That means that any value v_n of any variable X_n in the neighborhood is compatible with any value of the tuple t. By the construction of the JTT and according to Definition 2.13, any pairs of values in t and t' assigned to the same variable of the tuple, are compatible with the same values of the variables in the neighborhood. Thus, if a value x in tuple t is compatible with value v_n of the neighborhood, then also value x' in tuple t' in the same position as x [20] is also compatible with v_n. That, means one can interchange tuples t and t' in a solution and it will remain a solution. □

The above theorem proves interchangeability of two tuples containing values in the interchangeable set but does not prove that these values are interchangeable. In the above case they are interchangeable only in a certain context given by the assignments of the JTT node. As in Definition 2.9, they are interchangeable if for every tuple t containing one of them there is another tuple t' that admits the other such that t and t' are consistent with the same value combinations outside the dependent set. Thus, for every context there should exist a tuple of the dependent set for each value in the interchangeable set in order to be interchangeable.

We prove that as follows:

Lemma 2.3
The values in the interchangeable set are NTI with respect to the set S if and only if the JTT is compatible from the root node.

Proof. Note that in the JTT, tuples admissible for any node on the path from a node n to the root node are compatible with all assignments as tuples admissible for n. Thus, they can be substituted for tuples in n.

Consider a tuple t admissible at an arbitrary node n in the JTT. If the root of the JTT is compatible, there must be at least one node on the path from n to the root (including n) that contains a tuple for each value in the interchangeable set, and these tuples can be substituted for t.

---

[20]This means that x and x' are values assigned to the same variable X of the dependent set S with compatible tuples t and t'.

Conversely, assume that any tuple t can be substituted with some other tuple t' where the critical variables takes a different value in the interchangeable set. Then t' must be in the admissible tuples of a node on the path from the node where t is admissible to the root of the JTT. Now consider t' instead of t and continue until we reach a t that is admissible at a node such that no node above it has any admissible tuples. Then it can only be substituted with other tuples admissible at the same node, and the subtree at that node must be compatible. Thus, the JTT is compatible from its root node.   □

Lemma 2.4
If the root of the JTT is not compatible, and there is a value in the interchangeable set that does not occur in any of the admissible tuples of the nodes of the JTT, the values are not NTI for set S or any superset of set S.

Proof. In this case, there are tuples admissible for some node in the JTT that cannot be substituted by a tuple where the critical variable would take on the missing value because of inconsistencies in the set $S \cup \{X_i\}$. Consequently, the values cannot be NTI, and this will not change when the set S is enlarged.   □

Complexity of JTT Algorithm. Consider that we construct the JTT for a dependent set S of size s, and its corresponding JDT with a number k of leaves annotations. In the worse case, each leaf branch have to be compared to all the others in order to determine the relations in the JTT meaning a $O(k(k-1)/2)$ complexity and thus, $O(k^2)$. Moreover, the complexity for comparing two branch assignments is of $O(s \cdot d^2)$, where d is the largest domain size of variables in the assignments.

Algorithm for Searching Neighborhood Interchangeable Tuples (NTI)

In the following we describe the algorithm for computing the neighborhood partial interchangeable tuples, based on the JTT, Lemma 2.3 and Lemma 2.4.

This algorithm uses the algorithms described in the two previous subsections: DT (Algorithm 1), JDT (Algorithm 2) and JTT (Algorithm 7).

The algorithm NTI, see Algorithm 8, takes as input a critical variable X_i and an interchangeable set I. It determines a dependent set S of minimum size such that I is NTI with this dependent set. If no such set exists, it returns failure.

Algorithm 8 first computes the discrimination tree (DT) (see Algorithm 1.) to check whether I is neighborhood interchangeable. If this is the case, it returns with $S = \phi$. If not, it uses the DT to determine which variables to include in the initial candidate dependent set S. All assignments which place values in I in different branches in the DT must be included in any dependent set S for the NTI.

It then enters a search for a minimal dependent set S, considering them in the order of increasing size to ensure that the smallest is found first. For each

---

Algorithm 8: Procedure Neighborhood Tuple Interchangeability (NTI).
Input : critical variable X_i and interchangeable set I.

1: construct DT for X_i.
2: **if** interchangeable set values are NI **then**
3:     return (success, $S = \phi$).
4: **else**
5:     $S \leftarrow$ variables that are involved in DT assignments that are
        consistent with some values in the interchangeable set but not all.
6:     $OPEN \leftarrow (\{S\})$
7:     **repeat**
8:         $S \leftarrow first(OPEN), OPEN \leftarrow rest(OPEN)$.
9:         construct JDT for S.
10:        construct JTT.
11:        **if** root node compatible **then**
12:            return (success, S).
13:        **else**
14:            c $\leftarrow$ sets of minimal combinations of nodes of the JTT such
                that the union of their admissible tuples contains each value
                of the interchangeable set at least once.
15:            **for** c $\in$ C **do**
16:                $NS \leftarrow S \cup \bigcup_{n \in C}$. annotations of the arcs which are on the
                    path from root of JTT to node n.
17:                **if** $NS \notin OPEN$ **then**
18:                    include NS in $OPEN$ such that $OPEN$ is ordered in
                        increasing size.
19:        **until** $OPEN = \phi$
20: return failure.

---

candidate set, it computes first the JDT using Algorithm 2 and then the JTT using Algorithm 7. It then checks whether the JTT is compatible according to Definition 2.13. If it is, then S is a correct dependent set and the algorithm terminates.

If the JTT is not compatible, the algorithm generates all possible candidates for S that could provide a set of admissible tuples containing all values in the interchangeable set, and thus a compatible JTT. It adds these to the list of candidates, and continues with the next candidate.

Following the example given in Figure 2.17 subsection for the computation of tuple interchangeability for variable X_3 and its interchangeable set $I = \{t, v\}$, we can see in Figure 2.17 that the root node of the JTT obtained in the right side of the figure is not compatible. The consistent tuple we obtain from the root node annotation is only : $(X_3 = t, X_0 = v)$. As there is no consistent tuple for the other value v of the interchangeable set we have to start searching through the JTT for a consistent child node.

The first child node $X_0 = x$, gives the following consistent tuples: $(X_3 = t, X_0 = x)$, $(X_3 = t, X_0 = v)$, $(X_3 = v, X_0 = x)$ as we consider also the annotation in its parent when we compute the tuples.

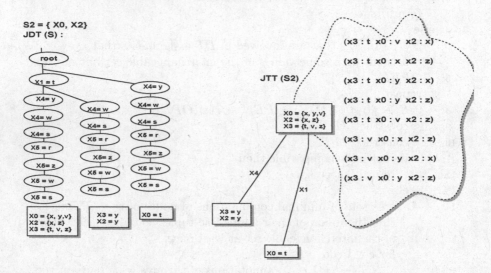

Figure 2.18: Joint Discrimination Tree (JDT) for the critical variable X_3, interchangeable set $I = \{t, v\}$ and dependent set $S_2 = \{X_0, X_2\}$ (left side). Joint Tuple Tree (JTT) for the critical variable X_3, interchangeable set $I = \{t, v\}$ and dependent set $S_2 = \{X_0, X_2\}$ (right side).

As we obtain at least one tuple for each value from the interchangeable set $I = \{t, v\}$, node $X_0 = x$ is consistent. As variable X_2 makes a difference between assignments of the root node and the child node $X_0 = x$, we have to include it in the dependent set S which now becomes $S_2 = \{X_0, X_2\}$ and reconstruct the JDT for the new S, see Figure 2.18. In fact, the new candidate sets are: $S_2 = \{X_0, X_2\}$ and $S_3 = \{X_0, X_2, X_4\}$ but we choose the smallest candidate first. This time the root node of the JTT is consistent as there is at least one consistent tuple for each value in the interchangeable set $I = \{t, v\}$.

The algorithm next examines the dependent set $S_2 = \{X_0, X_2\}$. The interchangeable tuples for the root node of the JTT are displayed in Figure 2.18. As it now has tuples for all $X_3 = t$ and $X_3 = v$, the root node is compatible and the algorithm terminates.

We display more results by applying the NTI algorithm for the variables of the problem in the Figure 2.1 in the Table 2.1.

We can see that for the critical variable X_0 and interchangeable set $I = \{x, y\}$, we obtained the dependent set $S = \{X_0, X_2\}$. For variable X_3 by interchanging values $\{t, z, q\}$, the dependent set obtained is $S = \{X_3, X_2, X_0\}$.

Critical variable X_0, $I = \{x, y\}$, $S = \{X_2\}$	Critical variable X_3, $I = \{t, z\}$, $S = \{X_2, X_0\}$	Critical variable X_3, $I = \{t, q\}$, $S = \{X_2, X_0\}$
$(X_0 = x, X_2 = y)$,	$(X_3 = t, X_2 = x, X_0 = y)$,	$(X_3 = t, X_2 = x, X_0 = y)$,
$(X_0 = x, X_2 = z)$,	$(X_3 = t, X_2 = y, X_0 = x)$,	$(X_3 = t, X_2 = x, X_0 = v)$,
$(X_0 = y, X_2 = x)$,	$(X_3 = t, X_2 = y, X_0 = v)$,	$(X_3 = t, X_2 = y, X_0 = x)$,
$(X_0 = y, X_2 = z)$	$(X_3 = t, X_2 = z, X_0 = x)$,	$(X_3 = t, X_2 = y, X_0 = v)$,
	$(X_3 = t, X_2 = z, X_0 = y)$,	$(X_3 = t, X_2 = z, X_0 = x)$,
	$(X_3 = t, X_2 = z, X_0 = v)$,	$(X_3 = t, X_2 = z, X_0 = y)$,
	$(X_3 = t, X_2 = q, X_0 = x)$,	$(X_3 = t, X_2 = z, X_0 = v)$,
	$(X_3 = t, X_2 = q, X_0 = y)$,	$(X_3 = t, X_2 = q, X_0 = x)$,
	$(X_3 = z, X_2 = q, X_0 = v)$,	$(X_3 = t, X_2 = q, X_0 = y)$,
	$(X_3 = z, X_2 = x, X_0 = y)$,	$(X_3 = t, X_2 = q, X_0 = v)$,
	$(X_3 = z, X_2 = x, X_0 = t)$,	$(X_3 = q, X_2 = x, X_0 = y)$,
	$(X_3 = z, X_2 = x, X_0 = v)$,	$(X_3 = q, X_2 = x, X_0 = t)$,
	$(X_3 = z, X_2 = y, X_0 = x)$,	$(X_3 = q, X_2 = x, X_0 = v)$,
	$(X_3 = z, X_2 = y, X_0 = t)$,	$(X_3 = q, X_2 = y, X_0 = x)$,
	$(X_3 = z, X_2 = y, X_0 = v)$,	$(X_3 = q, X_2 = y, X_0 = t)$,
	$(X_3 = z, X_2 = q, X_0 = y)$,	$(X_3 = q, X_2 = y, X_0 = v)$,
	$(X_3 = z, X_2 = q, X_0 = t)$,	$(X_3 = q, X_2 = z, X_0 = x)$,
	$(X_3 = z, X_2 = q, X_0 = v)$	$(X_3 = q, X_2 = z, X_0 = y)$,
		$(X_3 = q, X_2 = z, X_0 = t)$,
		$(X_3 = q, X_2 = z, X_0 = v)$

Table 2.1: Tuples at the root node of the JTT for different critical variables and interchangeable sets for the CSP of the Figure 2.1.

We can show:

Theorem 2.11

Algorithm 8 is sound: if it returns a dependent set S, then the set I is Neighborhood Tuple Interchangeable for the critical variable X_i.

Algorithm 8 is also complete: if the set I is NTI for X_i, then it will find a smallest dependent set S for this interchangeability.

Proof. Soundness follows from the fact that the algorithm checks compatibility of the JTT by Lemma 2.3 this is a sufficient condition for NTI.

Completeness follows from the fact that the algorithm checks all sets S that could satisfy the conditions of Lemma 2.3, and that the condition of Lemma 2.3 is also a necessary condition for NTI. Furthermore, when the set c becomes empty and there is no successor to a candidate S, then the algorithm has proven by Lemma 2.4 that there cannot be NTI with dependent set S or any superset of S, so it is not necessary to consider any possible indirect successors.

Furthermore, the dependent sets are considered in order of increasing size so that the first set that is found is guaranteed to be smallest.   □

We note that the algorithm could be adapted to return all possible minimal dependent sets for NTI by returning them one at a time in step 12 and continuing the algorithm until the list $OPEN$ becomes empty.

Generalization of NTI Algorithm

Solution update techniques can successfully apply the NTI algorithm in order to adapt solutions. The NTI algorithm input has as input variable X_i for which one might want to interchange the values in the interchangeable set $I = \{a, b\}$. The first straightforward generalization is to consider a subdomain of values that we want to interchange for variable $X_i : I = \{d_i \subseteq D_i\}$. In this case, the algorithm requires only slight modification in the its first part. It constructs the Discrimination Tree for variable X_i and the values from the interchangeable I. Further, it constructs the set S containing critical variable X_i and variables which make differences between DT branches assignments [21]. The algorithm continues as usual with JDT and JTT algorithms for the obtained set of variables S.

Algorithm 8 can be forward generalized having as input a set of critical variables $S = \{X_{i1}, X_{i2}, \ldots, X_{ik}\}$ and their subdomains of values to interchange, the interchangeable set $I = \{d_{i1}, \ldots, d_{ik}\}$. In a solution update method one might need to specify the variables he needs to update and the subdomains in which these variables can take values. Again, the algorithm has to be slightly modified only in the first part. Thus, it starts by constructing the JDT for the input set of critical variables taking only the values in the interchangeable set I. The set S is further extended with the variables making differences between all branches assignments and next the algorithm flows as usual with the JDT and JTT construction for the new S, searching for the minimal dependent set.

Complexity of NTI Algorithm

Most of the NTI algorithm complexity is generated by the computation of the structures used by it: DT, JDT and JTT. The complexity of DT and JDT algorithm are presented in the previous chapter, see Section 2.2. As presented in Section 2.3.3, the complexity is computed when we apply the DT algorithm for all the variables in the CSP, but in the NTI algorithm this complexity is reduced drastically as we compute, for only one variable and its two values, the size of the interchangeable set, of one critical variable from $O(n^2 \cdot d^2)$ to $O(n \cdot d)$, where n is the number of CSP variables and d the largest domain size. For the more generic case when the input is a set of critical variables and their subdomains to interchange, the complexity grows to $O(s \cdot n \cdot d \cdot d_i)$, where s is the size of the critical set and d_i

---

[21]As the DT is constructed only for values contained in the interchangeable set I of variable X_i, we consider all the branches of this DT to obtain the variables which differentiate them.

the largest subdomain, n and d as specified previously. Moreover, its complexity tends to be a function of the JDT structure computation: $O(s(n - s) \cdot d^2)$, where n is the size of the CSP, s is the size of the set S and d is the maximum domain size of variables.

As shown in worst cases scenarios, the complexity of the complete algorithm tends to be high but we can show experimentally that can be applied successfully in practice. In the following section we present how it works on a graph coloring example, present results on random generated problems and give heuristics which trade on completeness but can reduce on complexity.

2.6.3 Results

In this section we describe results obtained during an empirical study for NTI occurrence and spread in random generated problems. In order to understand when NTI appears and how it depends on the problem structure, we consider the four constraint problem parameters and tried to isolate them in terms of their effects on the tuple interchangeability. The problem characteristics on which we concentrate in our measurements were: the number of variables in the CSP, n, the maximum domain size of the variables, dom, the tightness of the constraints, t, and the constraint density, $dens$.

In our experiments, we measured two parameters of the NTI occurrence:

- the average tuple size per variable, Av_s;

- the average number of interchangeable tuples per variable, Av_t.

Both averages above are obtained by computing the sets of interchangeable tuples for each value pair of each variable normalized to the domain size of the variable.

The test were conducted in the following way: For each data point, we generated 20 random problems where CSP parameters on which we measure the variation are held constant at fixed points while the others are either fixed or randomly chosen as described in the following.

In Figure 2.19 we study the dependence of our two measures Av_s and Av_t on the problem density. For each data point we generated 20 random problems with the following parameters : $n = 10$, $dom = 10$, $dens$ vary for each point in the set $\{0.1, 0.3, \ldots, 0.9\}$ and t vary randomly in the interval $[0.1, 0.9]$. We can observe that both measures Av_s and Av_t do not vary with the CSP density.

In Figure 2.20 we study how the measures Av_s and Av_t vary with the CSP tightness. For each data point we generated 20 random problems with the following parameters : $n = 10$, $dom = 10$, $dens$ varies randomly in the interval $[0.1, 0.9]$ and t varies for each point in the set $\{0.1, 0.3, \ldots, 0.9\}$. We can observe that mDS set size increases with the CSP tightness. The number of interchangeable tuples appears not to be dependent on the CSP tightness. Note that we also count in our measurements tuples of one variable, thus the NI values.

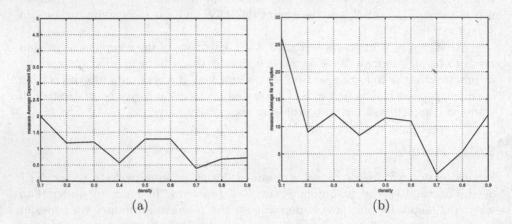

Figure 2.19: (a) The dependence of the interchangeable tuple size on the *CSP* density. (b) The dependence of the interchangeable tuple number on the CSP density.

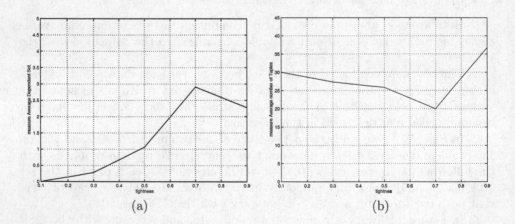

Figure 2.20: (a) The dependence of the interchangeable tuple size on the *CSP* tightness. (b) The dependence of the interchangeable tuple number on the *CSP* tightness.

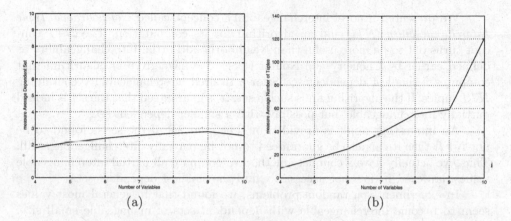

(a)   (b)

Figure 2.21: (a) The dependence of the interchangeable tuple size on the number of variables in the CSP. (b) The dependence of the interchangeable tuple number on the number of variables in the CSP.

In our experiments we measured as well the dependence of tuple occurrence on the problem size. For the results obtained in Figure 2.21, we generated random problems with the following parameters : n varies for each element in the set $\{4, .., 9, 10\}$, dom varies for each element in the set $\{4, .., 9, 10\}$, $dens$ varies randomly in the interval $[0.1, 0.9]$ and t varies randomly in the interval $[0.1, 0.9]$. In Figure 2.21(a), we can see that the interchangeable tuples size do not depend on the size of the problem, while the number of interchangeable tuples increases with the number of variables in the problem, see Figure 2.21(b).

From our empirical experimentation we derive the following conclusions:

- the interchangeable tuples size and their number do not depend on the CSP density;

- the interchangeable tuples size and their number increases with the CSP tightness, where the interchangeable tuples number is more sensitive to the CSP tightness;

- the interchangeable tuples size do not depend on the problem size, while the number of interchangeable tuples increases with the problem size. Both measures increase with the domain size.

2.6.4 Conclusions

In this work, we have developed algorithms for computing minimal, and the globally minimum dependent set which contains PI values/variables, and the first algorithm that allows finding of partial interchangeabilities without solving the entire problem.

We presented a novel interchangeability concept called *Neighborhood Tuple Interchangeability (NTI)* and an algorithm for its computation. The *NTI* concept turns out to be more useful than Neighborhood Partial Interchangeability as defined earlier by Choueiry and Noubir ([28]). We have given an algorithm that computes a smallest dependent set S for a desired interchangeability containing *NTI* tuples. If the algorithm finds such a set, it is guaranteed that the set is indeed partially interchangeable, but possibly with a smaller dependent set.

An interesting result is provided by Theorem 2.9: if the set is found to be not *NTI*, then it can also be guaranteed to not be partially interchangeable at all. Thus, we actually have a complete method to compute all partial interchangeable values; however, it does not necessarily find the smallest dependent sets.

In experiments on random problems, we found that in general most values seem to become interchangeable with dependent sets of manageable small size. Thus, while the complexity of our methods are exponential relative to the size of the dependent sets, we do not expect this to be a great problem in practice.

We have concentrated on computing *NTI* for a given critical variable and interchangeable set. In the future, it would be interesting to investigate if synergies can be obtained by computing *NTI* for all variables and domains in a single algorithm, in particular if it is possible to rapidly isolate those interchangeable sets for which the dependent sets are small.

Chapter 3

Interchangeability in Soft $CSPs$

The standard CSP framework proved to be generic but however has evident limitations. This framework appears to be not very flexible when trying to represent real life scenarios where the knowledge is not completely available nor crisp. For this reason the soft constraint framework has been defined. It allows to the classical notion of constraint the possibility of dealing with important features as fuzziness, uncertainty optimization, probability, and partial satisfaction.

In this work we define interchangeability in the Soft CSP framework, we give algorithms for its computation and study its occurrence and applicability.

3.1 Introduction

In many practical applications, constraints can be violated at a cost, and solving a CSP thus means finding a value assignment of minimum cost. Various frameworks for solving such soft constraints have been proposed [44, 34, 79, 38, 83, 14, 16, 8].

The soft constraints framework of c–semirings [14, 8] has been shown to express most of the known variants through different instantiations of its operators, and this is the framework we are considering in this work.

The most straightforward generalization of interchangeability to soft CSP would require that exchanging one value for another does not change the quality of the solution at all. This generalization is likely to suffer from the same weaknesses as interchangeability in hard CSP, namely that it is very rare.

Fortunately, soft constraints also allow weaker forms of interchangeability where exchanging values may result in a degradation of solution quality by some measure δ. By allowing more degradation, it is possible to increase the amount of interchangeability in a problem to the desired level. We define $^\delta$substitutability/interchangeability as a concept which ensures this quality. This is particularly useful when interchangeability is used for solution adaptation.

Another use of interchangeability is to reduce search complexity by grouping together values that would never give a sufficiently good solution. In $_\alpha$substitutability/interchangeability, we consider values interchangeable if they give equal solution quality in all solutions better than α, but possibly different quality for solutions whose quality is $\leq \alpha$.

We thus introduce two notions: *threshold* α and *degradation* δ for substitutability and interchangeability, ($_\alpha$substitutability/interchangeability and $^\delta$substitutability/interchangeability respectively). We show that they satisfy analogous theorems to the ones already known for hard constraints. In $_\alpha$interchangeability, values are interchangeable in any solution that is better than a threshold α, thus allowing to disregard differences among solutions that are not sufficiently good anyway. In $^\delta$interchangeability, values are interchangeable if their exchange could not degrade the solution by more than a factor of δ.

We give efficient algorithms to compute $(^\delta/_\alpha)$interchangeable sets of values for a large class of *SCSPs*.

Just like for hard constraints, full interchangeability is hard to compute, but can be approximated by neighborhood interchangeability which can be computed efficiently and implies full interchangeability. We define the same concepts for soft constraints, and prove that neighborhood implies full $(^\delta/_\alpha)$substitutability/interchangeability. We give algorithms for neighborhood $(^\delta/_\alpha)$substitutability/interchangeability, and we prove several interesting and useful properties of the concepts.

Finally, we give two examples where $(^\delta/_\alpha)$interchangeability is applied to solution adaptation in configuration problems with two different soft constraint frameworks: delay and cost constraints, and show its usefulness in these practical contexts.

3.2   Soft Constraint Satisfaction Problems (*SCSPs*)

Several formalization of the concept of *soft constraints* are currently available. In the following, we refer to the one based on c–semirings [8, 13, 14, 17], which can be shown to generalize and express many of the others [11, 12].

A soft constraint may be seen as a constraint where each instantiations of its variables has an associated value from a partially ordered set which can be interpreted as a set of preference values. Combining constraints will then have to take into account such additional values, and thus the formalism has also to provide suitable operations for combination ($\times$) and comparison ($+$) of tuples of values and constraints. This is why this formalization is based on the concept of c–semiring, which is just a set plus two operations.

Semirings.   A semiring is a tuple $\langle A, +, \times, \mathbf{0}, \mathbf{1} \rangle$ such that:

- A is a set and $\mathbf{0}, \mathbf{1} \in A$;

- $+$ is commutative, associative and $\mathbf{0}$ is its unit element;

- $\times$ is associative, distributes over $+$, $\mathbf{1}$ is its unit element and $\mathbf{0}$ is its absorbing element.

A c–semiring is a semiring $\langle A, +, \times, \mathbf{0}, \mathbf{1} \rangle$ such that: $+$ is idempotent, $\mathbf{1}$ is its absorbing element and $\times$ is commutative.

Let us consider the relation $\leq_S$ over A such that $a \leq_S b$ iff $a + b = b$. Then it is possible to prove that (see [14]):

- $\leq_S$ is a partial order;

- $+$ and $\times$ are monotone on $\leq_S$;

- $\mathbf{0}$ is its minimum and $\mathbf{1}$ its maximum;

- $\langle A, \leq_S \rangle$ is a complete lattice and, for all $a, b \in A$, $a + b = lub(a, b)$ (where *lub* is the *least upper bound*).

Moreover, if $\times$ is idempotent, then: $+$ distributes over $\times$; $\langle A, \leq_S \rangle$ is a complete distributive lattice and $\times$ its *glb* (*greatest lower bound*). Informally, the relation $\leq_S$ gives us a way to compare semiring values and constraints. In fact, when we have $a \leq_S b$, we will say that b *is better than* a. In the following, when the semiring will be clear from the context, $a \leq_S b$ will be often indicated by $a \leq b$.

Constraint Problems. Given a semiring $S = \langle A, +, \times, \mathbf{0}, \mathbf{1} \rangle$ and an ordered set of variables V over a finite domain D, a *constraint* is a function which, given an assignment $\eta : V \to D$ of the variables, returns a value of the semiring.

By using this notation we define $\mathcal{C} = \eta \to A$ as the set of all possible constraints that can be built starting from S, D and V.

Note that in this *functional* formulation, each constraint is a function (as defined in [17]) and not a pair (as defined in [13, 14]). Such a function involves all the variables in V, but it depends on the assignment of only a finite subset of them. So, for instance, a binary constraint $c_{x,y}$ over variables x and y, is a function $c_{x,y} : V \to D \to A$, but it depends only on the assignment of variables $\{x, y\} \subseteq V$. We call this subset the *support* of the constraint.

More formally, consider a constraint $c \in \mathcal{C}$. We define its support as $supp(c) = \{v \in V \mid \exists \eta, d_1, d_2 . c\eta[v := d_1] \neq c\eta[v := d_2]\}$, where

$$\eta[v := d]v' = \begin{cases} d & \text{if } v = v', \\ \eta v' & \text{otherwise.} \end{cases}$$

Note that $c\eta[v := d_1]$ means $c\eta'$ where η' is η modified with the assignment $v := d_1$ (that is the operator $[\,]$ has precedence over application). Note also that $c\eta$ is the application of a constraint function $c : V \to D \to A$ to a function $\eta : D \to A$; what we obtain, is a semiring value $c\eta = a$.

A *soft constraint satisfaction problem* is a pair $\langle C, con \rangle$ where $con \subseteq V$ and C is a set of constraints: con is the set of variables of interest for the constraint set C, which however may concern also variables not in con. Note that a classical CSP is a $SCSP$ where the chosen c–semiring is: $S_{CSP} = \langle \{false, true\}, \vee, \wedge, false, true \rangle$. Fuzzy $CSPs$ [81] can instead be modelled in the $SCSP$ framework by choosing the c–semiring $S_{FCSP} = \langle [0,1], max, min, 0, 1 \rangle$. Many other "soft" $CSPs$ (Probabilistic, weighted, ...) can be modelled by using a suitable semiring structure ($S_{prob} = \langle [0,1], max, \times, 0, 1 \rangle$, $S_{weight} = \langle \mathcal{R}, min, +, +\infty, 0 \rangle$, ...).

Fig. 3.1 shows the graph representation of a fuzzy CSP. Variables and constraints are represented respectively by nodes and by undirected (unary for c_1 and c_3 and binary for c_2) arcs, and semiring values are written to the right of the corresponding tuples. The variables of interest (that is the set con) are represented with a double circle. Here we assume that the domain D of the variables contains only elements a and b and c.

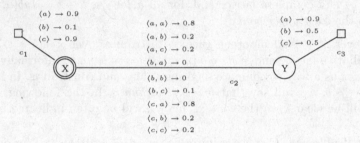

Figure 3.1: A fuzzy CSP.

Combining and projecting soft constraints. Given the set $\mathcal{C}$, the combination function $\otimes : \mathcal{C} \times \mathcal{C} \to \mathcal{C}$ is defined as $(c_1 \otimes c_2)\eta = c_1\eta \times_S c_2\eta$.

In words, combining two constraints means building a new constraint whose support involves all the variables of the original ones, and which associates with each tuple of domain values for such variables a semiring element which is obtained by multiplying the elements associated by the original constraints to the appropriate subtuples. It is easy to verify that $supp(c_1 \otimes c_2) \subseteq supp(c_1) \cup supp(c_2)$.

Given a constraint $c \in \mathcal{C}$ and a variable $v \in V$, the *projection* of c over $V - \{v\}$, written $c \Downarrow_{(V - \{v\})}$ is the constraint c' s.t. $c'\eta = \sum_{d \in D} c\eta[v := d]$. Informally, projecting means eliminating some variables from the support. This is done by associating with each tuple over the remaining variables a semiring element which is the sum of the elements associated by the original constraint to all the extensions of this tuple over the eliminated variables. In short, combination is performed via the multiplicative operation of the semiring, and projection via the additive one.

Solutions. A *solution* of an $SCSP$ $P = \langle C, con \rangle$ is the constraint $Sol(P) = (\bigotimes C) \Downarrow_{con}$. That is, we combine all constraints, and then project over the variables in con. In this way we get the constraint with support (not greater than) *con* which is "induced" by the entire $SCSP$. Note that when all the variables are of interest we do not need to perform any projection.

For example, the solution of the fuzzy CSP of Fig. 3.1 associates a semiring element to every domain value of variable x. Such an element is obtained by first combining all the constraints together. For instance, for the tuple $\langle a, a \rangle$ (that is, $x = y = a$), we have to compute the minimum between 0.9 (which is the value assigned to $x = a$ in constraint c_1), 0.8 (which is the value assigned to $\langle x = a, y = a \rangle$ in c_2) and 0.9 (which is the value for $y = a$ in c_3). Hence, the resulting value for this tuple is 0.8. We can do the same work for tuple $\langle a, b \rangle \rightarrow 0.2$, $\langle a, c \rangle \rightarrow 0.2$, $\langle b, a \rangle \rightarrow 0$, $\langle b, b \rangle \rightarrow 0$, $\langle b, c \rangle \rightarrow 0.1$, $\langle c, a \rangle \rightarrow 0.8$, $\langle c, b \rangle \rightarrow 0.2$ and $\langle c, c \rangle \rightarrow 0.2$. The obtained tuples are then projected over variable x, obtaining the solution $\langle a \rangle \rightarrow 0.8$, $\langle b \rangle \rightarrow 0.1$ and $\langle c \rangle \rightarrow 0.8$.

3.3 Defining Interchangeability in Soft $CSPs$

In soft $CSPs$, there is not any crisp notion of consistency. In fact, each tuple is a possible solution, but with different level of preference. Therefore, in this framework, the notion of interchangeability becomes finer: to say that values a and b are interchangeable we have also to consider the assigned semiring level.

More precisely, if a domain element a assigned to variable v can be substituted in each tuple solution with a domain element b without obtaining a worse semiring level we say that b is full substitutable for a.

Definition 3.1 (Full Substitutability (FS)) Consider two domain values b and a for a variable v, and the set of constraints C; we say that b is Full Substitutable for a on v ($b \in FS_v(a)$) if and only if

$$\bigotimes C\eta[v := a] \leq_S \bigotimes C\eta[v := b]$$

When we restrict this notion only to the set of constraints C_v that involves variable v we obtain a local version of substitutability.

Definition 3.2 (Neighborhood Substitutability (NS)) Consider two domain values b and a for a variable v, and the set of constraints C_v involving v; we say that b is neighborhood substitutable for a on v ($b \in NS_v(a)$) if and only if

$$\bigotimes C_v\eta[v := a] \leq_S \bigotimes C_v\eta[v := b]$$

When the relations hold in both directions, we have the notion of Full/Neighbourhood interchangeability of b with a.

Definition 3.3 (Full and Neighborhood Interchangeability (FI and NI)) Consider two domain values b and a, for a variable v, the set of all constraints C and the set of constraints C_v involving v. We say that b is fully interchangeable with a on v $(FI_v(a/b))$ if and only if $b \in FS_v(a)$ and $a \in FS_v(b)$, that is

$$\bigotimes C\eta[v := a] = \bigotimes C\eta[v := b].$$

We say that b is Neighborhood interchangeable with a on v $(NI_v(a/b))$ if and only if $b \in NS_v(a)$ and $a \in NS_v(b)$, that is

$$\bigotimes C_v\eta[v := a] = \bigotimes C_v\eta[v := b].$$

This means that when a and b are interchangeable for variable v they can be exchanged without affecting the level of any solution.

Two important results that hold in the crisp case can be proven to be satisfied also with soft $CSPs$: transitivity and extensivity of interchangeability/substitutability.

Theorem 3.1: Extensivity: $NS \implies FS$ **and** $NI \implies FI$.
Consider two domain values b and a for a variable v, the set of constraints C and the set of constraints C_v involving v. Then, neighborhood (substitutability) interchangeability implies full (substitutability) interchangeability.

Proof. By definition of neighborhood substitutability,

$$b \in NS_v(a) \iff \forall \eta, \bigotimes C_v\eta[v := a] \leq_S \bigotimes C_v\eta[v := b].$$

Now, since the assignments $v := a$ and $v := b$ only involve constraints in C_v, and for the extensivity properties of times, we easily have that

$$\forall \eta, \bigotimes C\eta[v := a] \leq_S \bigotimes C\eta[v := b],$$

that is $b \in FS_v(a)$. Easily, we can extend the result to interchangeability. □

Theorem 3.2: Transitivity: $b \in NS_v(a), a \in NS_v(c) \implies b \in NS_v(c)$.
Consider three domain values a, b and c, for a variable v. Then,

$$b \in NS_v(a), a \in NS_v(c) \implies b \in NS_v(c).$$

Similar results hold for FS, NI and FI.

Proof. By definition of neighborhood substitutability,

$$b \in NS_v(a) \iff \forall \eta, \bigotimes C_v\eta[v := a] \leq_S \bigotimes C_v\eta[v := b] \text{ and,}$$

$$a \in NS_v(c) \iff \forall \eta, \bigotimes C_v\eta[v := c] \leq_S \bigotimes C_v\eta[v := a].$$

Now, for transitivity of $\leq_S$, we easily have that

$$\forall \eta, \bigotimes C\eta[v := c] \leq_S \bigotimes C\eta[v := b],$$

that is $b \in NS_v(c)$. Easily, we can extend the result for FS, NI and FI.

$\square$

As an example of interchangeability and substitutability consider the fuzzy CSP represented in Fig. 3.1. The domain value c is neighborhood interchangeable with a on x ($NI_x(a/c)$); in fact, $c_1 \otimes c_2\eta[x := a] = c_1 \otimes c_2\eta[x := c]$ for all η.

The domain values c and a are also neighborhood substitutable for b on x ($\{a, c\} \in NS_v(b)$). In fact, for any η we have $c_1 \otimes c_2\eta[x := b] \leq c_1 \otimes c_2\eta[x := c]$ and $c_1 \otimes c_2\eta[x := b] \leq c_1 \otimes c_2\eta[x := a]$.

3.3.1 Relaxed Soft Interchangeability – Degradation and Threshold

In soft $CSPs$, any value assignment is a solution, but may have a very bad preference value. This allows broadening the original interchangeability concept to one that also allows degrading the solution quality when values are exchanged. We call this $^\delta$interchangeability, where δ is the *degradation* factor.

When searching for solutions to soft CSP, it is possible to gain efficiency by not distinguishing values that could in any case not be part of a solution of sufficient quality. In $_\alpha$interchangeability, two values are interchangeable if they do not affect the quality of any solution with quality better than α. We call α the *threshold* factor. Moreover, sometimes we are just looking for *any* solution greater than a certain level α. In this case, also the notion of $_\alpha$interchangeability could be too strict. For this motivation we define also a more relaxed notion of threshold that we call α−set.

Both concepts can be combined, i.e. we can allow both degradation and limit search to solutions better than a certain threshold ($_\alpha^\delta$interchangeability).

By extending the previous definitions we can define thresholds and degradation version of full/neighbourhood substitutability/interchangeability.

Definition 3.4 ($^\delta$Full/Neighbourhood Substitutability ($^\delta FS/NS$)) Consider two domain values b and a for a variable v, the set of constraints C and a semiring level δ; we say that b is $^\delta$*fully substitutable* for a on v ($b \in {}^\delta FS_v(a)$) if and only if for all assignments η,

$$\bigotimes C\eta[v := a] \times_S \delta \leq_S \bigotimes C\eta[v := b]$$

It is $^\delta$*neighborhood substitutable* if the condition holds for C being the subset of the constraints that have v as a variable.

Definition 3.5 ($_\alpha$Full Substitutability ($_\alpha FS$)) Consider two domain values b and a, for a variable v, the set of constraints C and a semiring level α; we say that b is $_\alpha$*full substitutable* for a on v ($b \in {}_\alpha FS_v(a)$) if and only if for all assignments η,

$$\bigotimes C\eta[v := a] \geq \alpha \implies \bigotimes C\eta[v := a] \leq_S \bigotimes C\eta[v := b]$$

Definition 3.6 ($_\alpha$Full/Neighbourhood Substitutability ($_\alpha FS/NS$)) Consider two domain values b and a, for a variable v, the set of constraints C and a semi-ring level α; we say that b is $_\alpha$*fully substitutable* for a on v ($b \in {_\alpha}FS_v(a)$) if and only if for all assignments η,

$$\bigotimes C\eta[v := a] \geq_S \alpha \implies \bigotimes C\eta[v := a] \leq_S \bigotimes C\eta[v := b]$$

It is $_\alpha$*neighborhood substitutable* if the condition holds for C being the subset of the constraints that have v as a variable.

Definition 3.7 ($_{\alpha-\text{set}}$Full/Neighbourhood Substitutability ($_{\alpha-\text{set}}FS/NS$)) Consider two domain values b and a, for a variable v, the set of constraints C and a semiring level α; we say that b is $_{\alpha-\text{set}}$*full substitutable* for a on v ($b \in {_{\alpha-\text{set}}}FS_v(a)$) if and only if for all assignments η,

$$\bigotimes C\eta[v := a] \geq_S \alpha \implies \bigotimes C\eta[v := b] \geq_S \alpha$$

It is $_{\alpha-\text{set}}$*neighborhood substitutable* if the condition holds for C being the subset of the constraints that have v as a variable.

Definition 3.8 (Full/Neighbourhood Soft Interchangeability) Consider two domain values b and a, for a variable v, the set of constraints C. Values a and b are

- $^\delta$*fully/neighbourhood interchangeable* iff they are $^\delta$*fully/neighbourhood substitutable* both ways.
- $_\alpha$*fully/neighbourhood interchangeable* iff they are $_\alpha$*fully/neighbourhood substitutable* both ways.
- $_{\alpha-\text{set}}$*fully/neighbourhood interchangeable* iff they are $_{\alpha-\text{set}}$*fully/neighbourhood substitutable* both ways.

    It is easy to see from the definition that

Theorem 3.3: $\alpha \implies \alpha-\text{set}$.
Consider two domain values a and b, for a variable v, and a thresholds α. Then,

$$a \in {_\alpha}NS_v(b) \implies a \in {_{\alpha-\text{set}}}NS_v(b)$$

Similar results holds for FS, NI, FI.

Proof. By definition of α and $\alpha-\text{set}$ substitutability,

$$b \in {_\alpha}FS_v(a) \iff$$
$$\forall \eta, \bigotimes C\eta[v := a] \geq_S \alpha \implies \bigotimes C\eta[v := a] \leq_S \bigotimes C\eta[v := b], \text{ and,}$$
$$b \in {_{\alpha-\text{set}}}FS_v(a) \iff$$
$$\forall \eta, \bigotimes C\eta[v := a] \geq_S \alpha \implies \bigotimes C\eta[v := b] \geq_S \alpha.$$

Now, when $\bigotimes C\eta[v := a] < \alpha$ both the clauses are true; when $\bigotimes C\eta[v := a] \geq_S \alpha$, by hypothesis, we have $\bigotimes C\eta[v := a] \leq_S \bigotimes C\eta[v := b]$. For transitivity, we easily have $\bigotimes C\eta[v := b] \geq_S \alpha$. We can extend the result for NS, NI and FI. $\quad\square$

As an example consider Fig. 3.1. The domain values c and b for variable y are $_{0.2}$Neighborhood Interchangeable. In fact, the tuple involving c and b only differ for the tuple $\langle b, c \rangle$ that has value 0.1 and for the tuple $\langle b, b \rangle$ that has value 0. Since we are interested only to solutions greater than 0.2, these tuples are excluded from the match.

We can see also that values a and b for variable y are $_{0.2-set}$Neighborhood. In fact the set of solution tuples with value greater than 0.2 are the same. Notice that a and b are not $_{0.2}$Neighborhood Interchangeable because tuples $\langle a, a \rangle$ and $\langle a, b \rangle$ have values 0.8 and 0.2 respectively.

The meaning of degradation assume different meanings when instantiated to different semirings:

1. fuzzy CSP: $b \in {}^{\delta}FS_v(a)$ gets instantiated to:

$$min(min_{c \in C}(c\eta[v := a]), \delta) \leq min_{c \in C}(c\eta[v := b])$$

which means that changing $v := b$ to $v := a$ does not make the solution worse than before or worse than δ. In the practical case where we want to only consider solutions with a quality better than δ, this means that substitution will never put a solution out of this class.

2. weighted CSP: $b \in {}^{\delta}FS_v(a)$ gets instantiated to:

$$\sum_{c \in C} c\eta[v := a] + \delta \geq \sum_{c \in C} c\eta[v := b]$$

which means that the penalty for the solution does not increase by more than a factor of δ. This allows for example to express that we would not want to tolerate more than δ in extra cost. Note, by the way, that $\leq_S$ translates to $\geq$ in this version of the soft CSP.

3. probabilistic CSP: $b \in {}^{\delta}FS_v(a)$ gets instantiated to:

$$\left(\prod_{c \in C} c\eta[v := a]\right) \cdot \delta \leq \prod_{c \in C} c\eta[v := b]$$

which means that the solution with $v = b$ is not degraded by more than a factor of δ from the one with $v = a$.

4. crisp CSP: $b \in {}^{\delta}FS_v(a)$ gets instantiated to:

$$\left(\bigwedge_{c \in C} c\eta[v := a]\right) \wedge \delta \Rightarrow \left(\bigwedge_{c \in C} c\eta[v := b]\right)$$

which means that when $\delta = true$, whenever a solution with $v = a$ satisfies all constraints, so does the same solution with $v = b$. When $\delta = false$, it is trivially satisfied (i.e. δ is too loose a bound to be meaningful).

This shows that the definitions correspond well to the intuitions, and allow us to tune the amount of substitutability/interchangeability by varying δ, with $\delta = 1$ being the strictest.

3.3.2 Properties of Degradations and Thresholds

As it is very complex to determine full interchangeability/substitutability, we start by showing the fundamental theorem that allows us to approximate $^\delta/_{\alpha/\alpha-\text{set}}FS/FI$ by $^\delta/_{\alpha/\alpha-\text{set}}NS/NI$:

Theorem 3.4: Extensivity.
$^\delta$neighborhood substitutability implies $^\delta$full substitutability, $_\alpha$neighborhood substitutability implies $_\alpha$full substitutability and $_{\alpha-\text{set}}$neighborhood substitutability implies $_{\alpha-\text{set}}$full substitutability..

Proof. • δ: Since the assignments $v := a$ and $v := b$ only involve constraints in C_v, and for the extensivity properties of times, we easily have that

$$b \in NS_v(a) \iff$$

$$\forall \eta, \bigotimes C_v\eta[v := a] \times_S \delta \leq_S \bigotimes C_v\eta[v := b]$$

$$\implies$$

$$\forall \eta, \bigotimes C\eta[v := a] \times_S \delta \leq_S \bigotimes C\eta[v := b]$$

$$\iff b \in FS_v(a).$$

• α: When $\bigotimes C_v\eta[v := a] < \alpha$ also $\bigotimes C\eta[v := a] < \alpha$, so both the clauses are true; when $\bigotimes C_v\eta[v := a] \geq_S \alpha$, since $\bigotimes C_v\eta[v := a] \leq_S \bigotimes C_v\eta[v := b]$, we have by extensivity $\bigotimes C\eta[v := a] \leq_S \bigotimes C\eta[v := b]$.

• $\alpha-$set: As before, when $\bigotimes C_v\eta[v := a] < \alpha$ also $\bigotimes C\eta[v := a] < \alpha$, so both the clauses are true. When $\bigotimes C_v\eta[v := a] \geq_S \alpha$, since by hypothesis $b \in _{\alpha-\text{set}}FS_v(a)$, I have $\bigotimes C_v\eta[v := b] \geq_S \alpha$; now per extensivity we have also $\bigotimes C\eta[v := b] \geq_S \alpha$.

Easily, we can extend the result to interchangeability.   □

This theorem is of fundamental importance since it gives us a way to approximate full interchangeability by neighborhood interchangeability which is much less expensive to compute.

Theorem 3.5: Transitivity using thresholds and degradations.
Consider three domain values a, b and c, for a variable v. Then,

$$b \in {}^{\delta_1}NS_v(a), a \in {}^{\delta_2}NS_v(c) \implies b \in {}^{\delta_1 \times \delta_2}NS_v(c) \text{ and}$$
$$b \in {}_{\alpha_1}NS_v(a), a \in {}_{\alpha_2}NS_v(c) \implies b \in {}_{\alpha_1+\alpha_2}NS_v(c).$$

Similar results holds for FS, NI, FI.

Proof. • δ: By definition

$$a \in {}^{\delta_2} NS_v(c) \iff \forall \eta, \bigotimes C_v \eta[v := c] \times_S \delta_2 \leq_S \bigotimes C_v \eta[v := a].$$

For monotonicity we have

$$\forall \eta, \bigotimes C_v \eta[v :- c] \times_S \delta_2 \times_S \delta_1 \leq_S \bigotimes C_v \eta[v := a] \times_S \delta_1.$$

Now, by definition

$$b \in {}^{\delta_1} NS_v(a) \iff \forall \eta, \bigotimes C_v \eta[v := a] \times_S \delta_1 \leq_S \bigotimes C_v \eta[v := b].$$

For transitivity we easily have

$$\forall \eta, \bigotimes C_v \eta[v := c] \times_S \delta_2 \times_S \delta_1 \leq_S \bigotimes C_v \eta[v := b] \iff b \in {}^{\delta_1 \times \delta_2} NS_v(c).$$

• α: By hypothesis we have

$$b \in {}_{\alpha_1} NS_v(a) \iff$$
$$\bigotimes C_v \eta[v := a] \geq_S \alpha_1 \implies \bigotimes C_v \eta[v := a] \leq_S \bigotimes C_v \eta[v := b] \text{ and,}$$
$$a \in {}_{\alpha_2} NS_v(c) \iff$$
$$\bigotimes C_v \eta[v := c] \geq_S \alpha_2 \implies \bigotimes C_v \eta[v := c] \leq_S \bigotimes C_v \eta[v := a].$$

Since $\alpha_1 + \alpha_2 \geq_S \alpha_1$ and $\alpha_1 + \alpha_2 \geq_S \alpha_2$ and transitivity of $\implies$, we have

$$\bigotimes C_v \eta[v := a] \geq_S \alpha_1 + \alpha_2 \implies \bigotimes C_v \eta[v := a] \leq_S \bigotimes C_v \eta[v := b] \text{ and,}$$
$$\bigotimes C_v \eta[v := c] \geq_S \alpha_1 + \alpha_2 \implies \bigotimes C_v \eta[v := c] \leq_S \bigotimes C_v \eta[v := a].$$

Now for transitivity of $\leq_S$, we have

$$\bigotimes C_v \eta[v := c] \geq_S \alpha_1 + \alpha_2 \implies \bigotimes C_v \eta[v := c] \leq_S \bigotimes C_v \eta[v := b]$$
$$\iff b \in {}_{\alpha_1 + \alpha_2} NS_v(c).$$

Easily, we can extend the result to FS, NI, FI. □

In particular when $\alpha_1 = \alpha_2 = \alpha$ and $\delta_1 = \delta_2 = \delta$ we have:

Corollary 3.1: Transitivity and equivalence classes.
Consider three domain values a, b and c, for a variable v. Then,

- Threshold interchangeability is a transitive relation, and partitions the set of values for a variable into equivalence classes, that is

$$b \in {}_\alpha NS_v(a), a \in {}_\alpha NS_v(c) \implies b \in {}_\alpha NS_v(c)$$
$${}_\alpha NI_v(b/a), {}_\alpha NI_v(a/c) \implies {}_\alpha NI_v(b/c)$$
$$b \in {}_{\alpha-set} NS_v(a), a \in {}_{\alpha-set} NS_v(c) \implies b \in {}_{\alpha-set} NS_v(c)$$
$${}_{\alpha-set} NI_v(b/a), {}_{\alpha-set} NI_v(a/c) \implies {}_{\alpha-set} NI_v(b/c).$$

- If the $\times_S$–operator is idempotent, then degradation interchangeability is a transitive relation, and partitions the set of values for a variable into equivalence classes, that is

$$b \in {}^\delta NS_v(a), a \in {}^\delta NS_v(c) \implies b \in {}^\delta NS_v(c)$$
$${}^\delta NI_v(b/a), {}^\delta NI_v(a/c) \implies {}^\delta NI_v(b/c).$$

Proof.   • δ: Suppose to have $delta_1 = \delta_2 = \delta$. Since times is idempotent, we have $\delta_1 \times \delta_2 = \delta$. Using the results of the previous theorem the corollary easily follows.

- α: Since when $alpha_1 = \alpha_2 = \alpha$ we have $\alpha_1 + \alpha_2 = \alpha$, the corollary easily follows from the previous theorem.

- α–set: By hypothesis we have

$$b \in {}_\alpha NS_v(a) \iff \bigotimes C\eta[v := a] \geq_S \alpha \implies \bigotimes C\eta[v := b] \geq_S \alpha \text{ and,}$$

$$a \in {}_\alpha NS_v(c) \iff \bigotimes C\eta[v := c] \geq_S \alpha \implies \bigotimes C\eta[v := a] \geq_S \alpha.$$

For transitivity of $\implies$, we have

$$\bigotimes C\eta[v := c] \geq_S \alpha \implies \bigotimes C\eta[v := a] \geq_S \alpha.$$

Interchangeability easily follows.   □

By using degradations and thresholds we have a nice way to decide when two domain values for a variable can be substitutable/interchangeable. In fact, by changing the α or δ parameter we can obtain different results.

In particular we can show that an extensivity results for the parameters hold. In fact, it is straightforward to notice that if two values are ${}^\delta_\alpha$substitutable, they have to be also ${}^{\delta'}_{\alpha'}$substitutable for any $\delta' \leq \delta$ and $\alpha' \geq \alpha$.

Theorem 3.6: Extensivity for α and δ.
Consider two domain values a and b, for a variable v, two thresholds α and α' s.t. $\alpha \leq \alpha'$ and two degradations δ and δ' s.t. $\delta \geq \delta'$. Then,

$$a \in {}^\delta NS_v(b) \implies a \in {}^{\delta'} NS_v(b) \text{ and } a \in {}_\alpha NS_v(b) \implies a \in {}_{\alpha'} NS_v(b)$$

Similar results holds for FS, NI, FI.

Proof. • δ: By definition

$$a \in {}^{\delta}NS_v(b) \iff \forall \eta, \bigotimes C_v \eta[v := b] \times_S \delta \leq_S \bigotimes C_v \eta[v := a].$$

By monotonicity of times, we have

$$\bigotimes C_v \eta[v := b] \times_S \delta' \leq_S \bigotimes C_v \eta[v := b] \times_S \delta.$$

By transitivity of $\leq_S$

$$\forall \eta, \bigotimes C_v \eta[v := b] \times_S \delta' \leq_S \bigotimes C_v \eta[v := a] \iff a \in {}^{\delta'}NS_v(b).$$

• α: By Definition we have

$$a \in {}_{\alpha}NS_v(b) \iff$$
$$\bigotimes C_v \eta[v := b] \geq_S \alpha \implies \bigotimes C_v \eta[v := b] \leq_S \bigotimes C_v \eta[v := a].$$

Since $\alpha' \geq_S \alpha$, we have

$$\bigotimes C_v \eta[v := b] \geq_S \alpha' \implies \bigotimes C_v \eta[v := b] \geq_S \alpha.$$

By Transitivity of $\implies$ we have

$$\bigotimes C_v \eta[v := b] \geq_S \alpha' \implies \bigotimes C_v \eta[v := b] \leq_S \bigotimes C_v \eta[v := a]$$
$$\iff a \in {}_{\alpha'}NS_v(b).$$

Easily, we can extend the result to FS, NI, FI. □

As a corollary when threshold and degradation are **0** or **1** we have some special results.

Corollary 3.2
When $\alpha = \mathbf{0}$ and $\delta = \mathbf{1}$, we obtain the non approximated versions of NS. When $\alpha = \mathbf{1}$ and $\delta = \mathbf{0}$, all domain values are substitutable.

$$\forall a, b, \ a \in {}_{\mathbf{0}}NS_v(b) \text{ and } a \in {}^{\mathbf{1}}NS_v(b) \iff a \in NS(b)$$
$$\forall a, b, \ a \in {}_{\mathbf{1}}NS_v(b) \text{ and } a \in {}^{\mathbf{0}}NS_v(b).$$

Similar results holds for FS, NI, FI.

Proof. • When $\alpha = \mathbf{0}$, we always have $\bigotimes C_v \eta[v := b] \geq_S \alpha$. So to check if $a \in {}_{\mathbf{0}}NS_v(b)$ we need only to check that $\bigotimes C_v \eta[v := b] \leq_S \bigotimes C_v \eta[v := a]$.

• When $\delta = \mathbf{1}$, we have $\bigotimes C_v \eta[v := b] \times_S \delta = \bigotimes C_v \eta[v := b]$. So to check if $a \in {}^{\mathbf{1}}NS_v(b)$ we need only to check that $\bigotimes C_v \eta[v := b] \leq_S \bigotimes C_v \eta[v := a]$.

□

Let us remind that degradations and thresholds can be used together; so we easily have

- $_0^1 NS = {}_0 NS = {}^1 NS = NS$;

- $NS \implies {}^\delta NS \implies {}_\alpha^\delta NS$ for any δ and α;

- $NS \implies {}_\alpha NS \implies {}_\alpha^\delta NS$ for any δ and α.

3.4 Algorithms for Computing Interchangeability in Soft $CSPs$

The result of Theorem 3.1 is fundamental since it gives us a way to approximate full substituability/interchangeability by neighborhood substituability/interchangeability which is much less costly to compute.

The most general algorithm for neighborhood substituability/interchangeability in the soft CSP framework is to check for each pair of values whether the condition given in the definition holds or not. This algorithm has a time complexity exponential in the size of the neighborhood and quadratic in the size of the domain (which may not be a problem when neighborhoods are small).

Better algorithms can be given when the times operator of the semiring is idempotent. In this case, instead of considering the combination of all the constraint C_v involving a certain variable v, we can check the property we need (NS/NI and their relaxed versions $_\alpha^\delta NS/NI$) on each constraint itself.

Theorem 3.7

Consider two domain values b and a, for a variable v, and the set of constraints C_v involving v. Then we have $\forall c \in C_v$:

$$c\eta[v := a] \leq_S c\eta[v := b] \implies b \in NS_v(a) \tag{3.1}$$

$$(c\eta[v := a] \geq_S \alpha \implies c\eta[v := a] \leq_S c\eta[v := b]) \implies b \in {}_\alpha NS_v(a). \tag{3.2}$$

If the times operator of the semiring is idempotent we also have:

$$\forall c \in C_v . c\eta[v := a] \times_S \delta \leq_S c\eta[v := b] \implies b \in {}^\delta NS_v(a) \tag{3.3}$$

$$(c\eta[v := a] \geq_S \alpha \implies c\eta[v := b] \geq_S \alpha) \implies b \in {}_{\alpha-\text{set}} NS_v(a). \tag{3.4}$$

Proof.   1. Easily follows from the monotonicity of times.

2. For extensivity of times we have $\bigotimes C_v \eta[v := a] \leq_S \alpha \implies c\eta[v := a] \geq_S \alpha$. For monotonicity of times we have $c\eta[v := a] \leq_S c\eta[v := b] \implies \bigotimes C_v \eta[v := a] \leq_S \bigotimes C_v \eta[v := b]$. The thesis follows from transitivity of $\implies$.

3. For extensivity of times we have $\bigotimes C_v \eta[v := a] \leq_S \alpha \implies c\eta[v := a] \geq_S \alpha$. For monotonicity and idempotency of times we have $c\eta[v := a] \leq_S \alpha \implies \bigotimes C_v \eta[v := a] \leq_S \alpha$. The thesis follows from transitivity of $\implies$.

4. Easily follows from monotonicity and idempotency of times. □

By using Theorem 3.7 (and Corollary 3.1 for $^{\delta}/_{\alpha/\alpha-\text{set}}NS$) we can find substitutable/interchangeable domain values more efficiently. Algorithm 9 shows an algorithm that can be used to find domain values that are Neighborhood Interchangeable. It uses a data structure similar to the *discrimination trees*.

Algorithm 9: Algorithm to compute neighborhood interchangeable sets for variable v_i.

1: Create the root of the discrimination tree for variable v_i
2: Let $C_{v_i} = \{c \in C \mid v_i \in supp(c)\}$
3: Let $D_{v_i} = \{\text{the set of domain values } d_{v_i} \text{ for variable } v_i\}$
4: **for all** $d_{v_i} \in D_{v_i}$ **do**
5:    **for all** $c \in C_v$ **do**
6:       execute Algorithm NI–Nodes(c, v, d_{v_i}) to build the nodes associated with c
7:    Go back to the root of the discrimination tree.

Algorithm 9 can compute different versions of neighborhood interchangeability depending on the algorithm $NI - nodes$ used. Algorithm 10 shows the simplest version without threshold or degradation.

Algorithm 10: NI–Nodes(c, v, d_{v_i}) for Soft–NI.

1: **for all** assignments η_c to variables in $supp(c)$ **do**
2:    compute the semiring level $\beta = c\eta_c[v_i := d_{v_i}]$,
3:    **if** there exists a child node corresponding to $\langle c = \eta_c, \beta \rangle$ **then**
4:       move to it,
5:    **else**
6:       construct such a node and move to it.
7: Add $v_i, \{d_{v_i}\}$ to annotation of the last build node,

---

We can show that Algorithm 9 with procedure Algorithm 10 is sound (that is compute correct classes of equivalence for NI.

Theorem 3.8: Soundness of NI algorithm.
Algorithm 9 using Algorithm 10 returns as a result a subset of the neighborhood interchangeable sets.

Proof. By looking at Algorithm 10, two domain values d_{v_i} and d'_{v_i} will be in the same leaf node, if and only if they follow the same path. They follow the same path if and only if for all η, and for all $c \in C$, $c\eta[v_i := d_{v_i}] = c\eta[v_i := d'_{v_i}]$. This can be rewritten as $c\eta[v_i := d_{v_i}] \leq_S c\eta[v_i := d'_{v_i}]$ and $c\eta[v_i := d'_{v_i}] \leq_S c\eta[v_i := d_{v_i}]$.

Now by Theorem 3.7 this is equivalent to $d_{v_i} \in NS_{v_i}(d'_{v_i})$ and $d'_{v_i} \in NS_{v_i}(d_{v_i})$, that is $NI_{v_i}(d_{v_i}/d'_{v_i})$. $\square$

The Algorithm 10 is similar to that defined by Freuder in [42], and when we consider the semiring for classical $CSPs$ $S_{CSP} = \langle \{false, true\}, \vee, \wedge, false, true \rangle$ and all constraints are binary, it computes the same result. Notice that for each node we add also an information representing the cost of the assignment η_c.

When all constraints are binary, considering all constraints involving variable v is the same as considering all variables connected to v by a constraint, and our algorithm performs steps as that given by Freuder.

We can determine the complexity of the algorithm by considering that the algorithm calls $NI - Nodes$ for each $k - -ary$ constraint exactly once for each value of each the k variables; this can be bounded from above by $k * d$ with d the maximum domain size. Thus, given m constraints, we obtain a bound of

$$O(m * k * d * O(Algorithm NI - nodes)).$$

The complexity of $Algorithm NI - nodes$ strictly depends on the size of the domain d and from the number of variables k involved in each constraint and is given as

$$O(Algorithm NI - nodes) = d^{k-1}.$$

For complete constraint graphs of binary constraints ($k = 2$), we obtain the same complexity bound of $O(n^2 d^2)$ as Freuder in [42].

Algorithm 11: NI–Nodes(c, v, d_{v_i}) for Soft $_\alpha NI$.

1: **for all** assignments η_c to variables in $supp(c)$ s.t. $\beta = c\eta_c[v_i := d_{v_i}]$ and
   $\alpha \leq_S \beta$ **do**
2:     **if** there exists a child node corresponding to $\langle c = \eta_c, \beta \rangle$ **then**
3:         move to it,
4:     **else**
5:         construct such a node and move to it.
6: Add $v_i, \{d_{v_i}\}$ to annotation of the last build node,

---

Algorithms for the relaxed versions of NI are obtained by substituting different versions of Algorithm 10. For $_\alpha NI$, the algorithm needs to only consider tuples whose semiring value is greater than α, as shown in Algorithm 11.

Theorem 3.9: Soundness of the $_\alpha NI$ algorithm.
Algorithm 9 using Algorithm 11 returns as a result a subset of the $_\alpha$Neighborhood interchangeable values.

Proof. By looking at Algorithm 11, two domain values d_{v_i} and d'_{v_i} will be in the same leaf node, if and only if they follow the same path. They follow the same path if and only if for all η, and for all $c \in C$,

- both $c\eta[v_i := d_{v_i}]$ and $c\eta[v_i := d'_{v_i}]$ have a semiring value less than α, or

- $c\eta[v_i := d_{v_i}] = c\eta[v_i := d'_{v_i}]$

This can be written as:

$$(\neg(c\eta[v_i := d_{v_i}] \geq \alpha) \wedge \neg(c\eta[v_i := d'_{v_i}] \geq \alpha)) \vee (c\eta[v_i := d_{v_i}] = c\eta[v_i := d'_{v_i}]) \quad (3.5)$$

which, by distributing the first two terms, is equivalent to:

$$c\eta[v_i := d_{v_i}] \geq \alpha \implies (c\eta[v_i := d_{v_i}] \leq c\eta[v_i := d'_{v_i}])$$
$$\wedge$$
$$c\eta[v_i := d'_{v_i}] \geq \alpha \implies (c\eta[v_i := d'_{v_i}] \leq c\eta[v_i := d_{v_i}]).$$

Now by Theorem 3.7 this implies $d_{v_i} \in {}_\alpha NS_{v_i}(d'_{v_i})$ and $d'_{v_i} \in {}_\alpha NS_{v_i}(d_{v_i})$, that is ${}_\alpha NI_{v_i}(d_{v_i}/d'_{v_i})$. $\qquad\square$

Algorithm 12: NI–Nodes(c, v, d_{v_i}, α) for Soft ${}_{\alpha-\mathrm{set}} NI$.

1: **for all** assignments η_c to variables in $supp(c)$ **do**
2:     compute the semiring level $\beta = c\eta_c[v_i := d_{v_i}]$,
3:     **if** $\beta \not\geq \alpha$ **then**
4:         $\beta := \alpha$ {I do not want to discriminate in this case},
5:     **else**
6:         $\beta := \alpha$ {Does not matter how bigger than α}.
7:     **if** there exists a child node corresponding to $\langle c = \eta_c, \beta \rangle$ **then**
8:         move to it,
9:     **else**
10:       construct such a node and move to it.
11: Add $v_i, \{d_{v_i}\}$ to annotation of the last build node,

---

In Algorithm 12 instead, we have to filter out the tuples whose semiring value is lower than α and we do not make any difference among tuples greater than α.

Theorem 3.10: Soundness of ${}_{\alpha-\mathrm{set}} NI$ algorithm.
For semiring with idempotent $\times$–operator, Algorithm 9 using Algorithm 12 returns as result a subset of the ${}_{\alpha-\mathrm{set}}$Neighborhood interchangeable values.

Proof. By looking at Algorithm 12, two domain values d_{v_i} and d'_{v_i} will be in the same leaf node, only if they follow the same path. If they follow the same path, means that for all η, and for all $c \in C$,

- both $c\eta[v_i := d_{v_i}]$ and $c\eta[v_i := d'_{v_i}]$ have a semiring value not greater than α, or

- both have to be bigger than α.

This is is written as:

$$\neg((c\eta[v_i := d_{v_i}] \geq \alpha) \vee (c\eta[v_i := d'_{v_i}] \geq \alpha))$$
$$\vee$$
$$(c\eta[v_i := d_{v_i}] \geq \alpha) \wedge (c\eta[v_i := d'_{v_i}] \geq \alpha).$$

which by distributions transforms into:

$$(\neg(c\eta[v_i := d_{v_i}] \geq \alpha) \vee (c\eta[v_i := d_{v_i}] \geq \alpha)) \wedge$$
$$(\neg(c\eta[v_i := d_{v_i}] \geq \alpha) \vee (c\eta[v_i := d'_{v_i}] \geq \alpha)) \wedge$$
$$(\neg(c\eta[v_i := d'_{v_i}] \geq \alpha) \vee (c\eta[v_i := d_{v_i}] \geq \alpha)) \wedge$$
$$(\neg(c\eta[v_i := d'_{v_i}] \geq \alpha) \vee (c\eta[v_i := d'_{v_i}] \geq \alpha))$$

and by elimination of tautologies:

$$(\neg(c\eta[v_i := d_{v_i}] \geq \alpha) \vee (c\eta[v_i := d'_{v_i}] \geq \alpha)) \wedge$$
$$(\neg(c\eta[v_i := d'_{v_i}] \geq \alpha) \vee (c\eta[v_i := d_{v_i}] \geq \alpha))$$

Using the fact that $a \implies B \equiv \neg A \vee B$ this can be rewritten as:

$$((c\eta[v_i := d_{v_i}] \geq \alpha) \implies (c\eta[v_i := d'_{v_i}] \geq \alpha)) \wedge$$
$$((c\eta[v_i := d'_{v_i}] \geq \alpha) \implies (c\eta[v_i := d_{v_i}] \geq \alpha)).$$

Now by Theorem 3.7 this means that $d_{v_i} \in {}_{\alpha-set}NS_{v_i}(d'_{v_i})$ and $d'_{v_i} \in {}_{\alpha-set}NS_{v_i}(d_{v_i})$, that is ${}_{\alpha-set}NI_{v_i}(d_{v_i}/d'_{v_i})$.   □

Algorithm 13: NI–Nodes(c, v, d_{v_i}, δ) for Soft ${}^\delta NI$.

1: **for all** assignments η_c to variables in $supp(c)$ **do**
2:      compute the level $\beta = c\eta_c[v_i := d_{v_i}]$, and the bound $\kappa = \beta \times \delta$,
3:      **if** there exists a child node corresponding to $\langle \bar{\kappa}, (c = \eta_c), \bar{\beta} \rangle$ with $(\bar{\kappa} \leq \beta) \wedge (\kappa \leq \bar{\beta})$ **then**
4:          move to it and change the label to $\langle lub(\bar{\kappa}, \kappa), (c = \eta_c), glb(\bar{\beta}, \beta) \rangle$,
5:      **else**
6:          construct the node $\langle \kappa, (c = \eta_c), \beta \rangle$ and move to it.
7: Add $v_i, \{d_{v_i}\}$ to annotation of the last build node,

---

For ${}^\delta NI$, the algorithm needs to only consider tuples that can cause a degradation by more than δ, as shown in Algorithm 13. The idea here is to save in each node the information needed to check at each step ${}^\delta NS$ in both directions. In a semiring with total order, the information represent the 'interval of degradation'. As both algorithms consider the same assignments as Algorithm 10, their complexity remains unchanged at $O(d^{k-1})$.

Theorem 3.11: Soundness of the $^\delta NI$ algorithm.
For semirings with idempotent $\times$ operator, Algorithm 9 using Algorithm 13 gives as result a subset of the $^\delta$interchangeabilities.

Proof. By looking at Algorithm 13, two domain values d_{v_i} and d'_{v_i} will be in the same leaf node if and only if they follow the same path. Consider now for each node related to constraint c and to the assignment η, $c\eta_c[v_i := d_{v_i}] = \beta$, $\kappa = \beta \times \delta$, $c\eta_c[v_i := d'_{v_i}] = \beta'$, and $\kappa' = \beta' \times \delta$. If they follow the same path, each of the nodes will have a label $\langle lub(\bar{\kappa}, \kappa, \kappa'), c = \eta_c, glb(\bar{\beta}, \beta, \beta') \rangle$, where $\bar{\kappa}$ and $\bar{\beta}$ are determined by other assignments that have passed through the node.

Because of the condition in step 3 of Algorithm 13, the algorithm ensures that $lub(\bar{\kappa}, \kappa, \kappa') \leq glb(\bar{\beta}, \beta, \beta')$. It follows that $(\kappa' \leq \beta)$ and $\kappa \leq \beta'$.

By Theorem 3.7 this means that $d_{v_i} \in {}^\delta NS_{v_i}(d'_{v_i})$ and $d'_{v_i} \in {}^\delta NS_{v_i}(d_{v_i})$, that is $^\delta NI_{v_i}(d_{v_i}/d'_{v_i})$. $\qquad\square$

3.5 Soft Constraint Satisfaction for Configuration

Fig. 3.2 shows the graph representation of a CSP which might represent a car configuration problem.

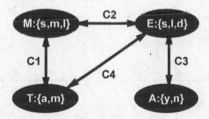

Figure 3.2: Example of a CSP modeling car configuration. It has 4 variables: $M = $ model, $T = $ transmission, $A = $ Air Conditioning, $E = $ Engine.

A product catalog might represent the available choices through a soft CSP. With different choices of semiring, the CSP of Fig. 3.2 can represent different problem formulations:

Example 21 For optimizing the cost of the product, a representation as a weighted CSP might be most appropriate. Here, the semiring models the cost of the different options and their integration with the others, using the semiring: $< \Re^+, min, +, +\infty, 0 >$. We might have the constraints:

$$
C_1 = \begin{array}{c|ccc} & \multicolumn{3}{c}{M} \\ & & s & m & l \\ \hline T & a & \infty & 5 & 3 \\ & m & 2 & 3 & 50 \end{array}
\qquad
C_2 = \begin{array}{c|ccc} & \multicolumn{3}{c}{M} \\ & & s & m & l \\ \hline E & s & 3 & 5 & \infty \\ & l & 30 & 3 & 3 \\ & d & 5 & 5 & \infty \end{array}
$$

$$C_3 = \begin{array}{c|ccc} & \multicolumn{3}{c}{E} \\ & s & l & d \\ \hline A \quad y & 5 & 2 & 7 \\ n & 0 & 30 & 0 \end{array} \qquad C_4 = \begin{array}{c|ccc} & \multicolumn{3}{c}{E} \\ & s & l & d \\ \hline T \quad a & \infty & 3 & \infty \\ m & 4 & 10 & 5 \end{array}$$

and also unary constraints C_M, C_E, C_T and C_A that model the cost of the components:

$$C_M = \begin{array}{ccc} s & m & l \\ \hline 10 & 20 & 30 \end{array} \quad C_E = \begin{array}{ccc} s & l & d \\ \hline 10 & 20 & 20 \end{array} \quad C_T = \begin{array}{cc} a & m \\ \hline 15 & 10 \end{array} \quad C_A = \begin{array}{cc} y & n \\ \hline 10 & 0 \end{array}$$

Example 22 Another optimization criterion might be the time it takes to build the car. Delay is determined by the time it takes to obtain the components and to reserve the resources for the assembly process. For the delivery time of the car, only the longest delay would matter. This could be modelled by the semiring $< \Re^+, min, max, +\infty, 0 >$[1], with the binary constraints:

$$C_1 = \begin{array}{c|ccc} & \multicolumn{3}{c}{M} \\ & s & m & l \\ \hline T \quad a & \infty & 3 & 4 \\ m & 2 & 4 & \infty \end{array} \qquad C_2 = \begin{array}{c|ccc} & \multicolumn{3}{c}{M} \\ & s & m & l \\ \hline \quad s & 2 & 3 & \infty \\ E \quad l & 30 & 3 & 3 \\ d & 2 & 3 & \infty \end{array}$$

$$C_3 = \begin{array}{c|ccc} & \multicolumn{3}{c}{E} \\ & s & l & d \\ \hline A \quad y & 5 & 4 & 7 \\ n & 0 & 30 & 0 \end{array} \qquad C_4 = \begin{array}{c|ccc} & \multicolumn{3}{c}{E} \\ & s & l & d \\ \hline T \quad a & \infty & 3 & \infty \\ m & 4 & 10 & 3 \end{array}$$

and unary constraints C_M, C_E, C_T and C_A that model the time to obtain the components:

$$C_M = \begin{array}{ccc} s & m & l \\ \hline 2 & 3 & 3 \end{array} \quad C_E = \begin{array}{ccc} s & l & d \\ \hline 3 & 2 & 3 \end{array} \quad C_T = \begin{array}{cc} a & m \\ \hline 1 & 2 \end{array} \quad C_A = \begin{array}{cc} y & n \\ \hline 3 & 0 \end{array}$$

Let us now consider the variable E of Example 3.5 and compute $^\delta/_\alpha NS/NI$ between its values by using Definition 3.4 and Definition 3.6. In Fig. 3.3 directed arcs are added when the source can be $^\delta/_\alpha$substituted to the destination node. It is easy to see how the occurrences of $^\delta/_\alpha NS$ change, depending on δ and α degrees.

We can notice that when δ takes value 0 (the **1** of the optimization semiring), small degradation is allowed in the CSP tuples when the values are substituted; thus only value s can be substituted for value d. As δ increases in value (or decreases from the semiring point of view) higher degradation of the solutions is allowed and thus the number of substitutable values increase with it.

---

[1]This semiring and the fuzzy one are similar, but the first uses an opposite order. Let us call this semiring *opposite–fuzzy*.

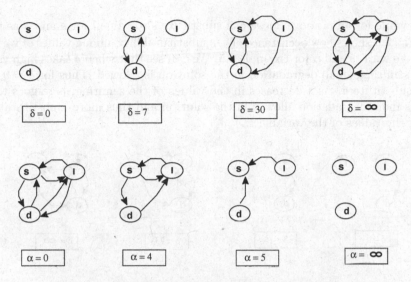

Figure 3.3: Example of how δ–substitutability and α–substitutability varies in the opposite–fuzzy CSP over the values of variable E.

In the second part of Fig. 3.3 we can see that for $\alpha = 0$ all the values are interchangeable (in fact, since there are no solutions better than $\alpha = 0$, by definition all the elements are $_\alpha$interchangeable).

For a certain threshold ($\alpha = 4$) values s and d are $_\alpha$interchangeable and value l can substitute values s and d. Moreover, when α is greater than 5 we only have that s can substitute d.

Further we consider the same variable E of the Example 3.5 for fuzzy CSP case and compute $_{\alpha-set}NS/NI$ by using the definition Definition 3.6. In Fig. 3.7, we can see how the occurrence of $_{\alpha-set}NS$ varies depending on the threshold α.

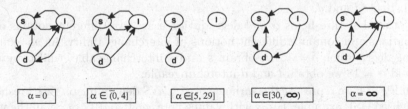

Figure 3.4: Example of how α–set–substitutability varies in the opposite–fuzzy CSP over the values of variable E from Fig. 3.2.

When α takes value 0 or ∞ all the values of variable E are $_{\alpha-set}interchangeable$. When value of alpha varies between value 0 and 4 value s is $_{\alpha-set}interchangeable$ with values l and d, where only d can be $_{\alpha-set}substitutable$ for value l. For an α higher then 4 and up to 29 we can interchange only values s

and d, while for an α above 30 we can substitute also value l for s and d as well.

Fig. 3.5 shows how occurrence of $^\delta/_\alpha$substitutability among values of variable E change w.r.t. δ and α for Example 3.5. We can see that when δ takes high values of the semiring, small degradation in the solution is allowed. Thus for $\delta = 0$ only s can substitute d. As δ decreases in the values of the semiring, here goes to ∞, there is more degradation allowed in the solution and thus more $^\delta$substitutability among the values of the variable E.

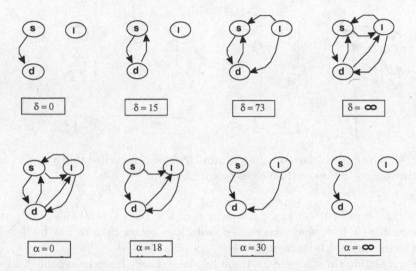

Figure 3.5: Example of how δ–substitutability and α–substitutability varies in the weighted CSP over the values of variable E from Fig. 3.2.

Let's now consider the second part of Fig. 3.5. For high semiring values of α all the values are interchangeable. For $\alpha = 18$ d and l are interchangeable, and s can substitute l and d.

Notice that thresholds α and degradation δ are two different notions of approximations and compute different notions of interchangeability. As an example, by using degradation $\delta = 15$ we obtain s and d interchangeable, whilst, by using threshold $\alpha = 18$ we obtain l and d interchangeable.

In Fig. 3.6 we represent the variance of $_{\alpha-set}NS$ depending on the threshold α for weighted CSP example. For α with values between 0 and 17 or ∞ all the values are $_{\alpha-set}interchangeable$. The number of $_{\alpha-set}substitutable$ values is decreasing with α till when $\alpha = 36$ and increasing again after all. It is interesting to notice that for this example that value s is always $_{\alpha-set}substitutable$ with value d; value l is $_{\alpha-set}substitutable$ to value s until α reaches value 28, while for value of α higher than 90, value l becomes $_{\alpha-set}substitutable$ for value s.

We will show now how to compute interchangeable values by using the Discrimination Tree algorithm. In Fig. 3.7 the Discrimination Tree is described for

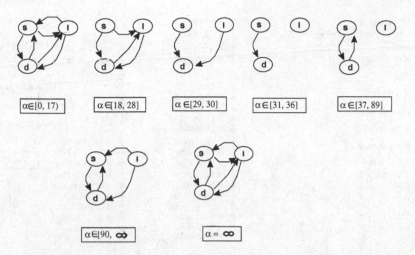

$\alpha \in [0, 17)$ $\alpha \in [18, 28]$ $\alpha \in [29, 30]$ $\alpha \in [31, 36]$ $\alpha \in [37, 89]$

$\alpha \in [90, \infty)$ $\alpha = \infty$

Figure 3.6: Example of how α–set–substitutability varies in the weighted CSP over the values of variable E from Fig. 3.2.

variable M when $\alpha = 2$ and $\alpha = 3$. We can see that values m and l for variable M are $_2$interchangeable whilst there are no interchangeabilities for $\alpha = 3$.

3.6 Experimental results

Occurrence of NI in classical CSP have been already studied to improve search [5], for resource allocation application [25] and for configuration problems [68]. One of the main result is that in problems of small density the number of NI sets increases with the domain size.

The behavior of NI sets in the Soft CSP frameworks is still unexploited. For this motivation we study and evaluate here how NI behaves in the Soft CSP framework.

We have done our experiments for fuzzy and weighted CSP representing the important class of Soft $CSPs$ dealing with an idempotent and non–idempotent times operation respectively. The motivation for considering both classes come from the fact that solving Soft CSP when the combination operation is not idempotent is extremely hard [14].

Usually the structure of a problem is characterized by four parameters:
- *Problem Size*: This is usually the number of its variables;
- *Domain Size*: The average of the cardinality of the domain of the variables;
- *Problem Density*: This value (measured on the interval [0,1]) is the ratio of the number of constraints relatively to the minimum and maximum number of allowed constraints in the given problem; Considering the constraint problem as a constraint graph $G = (V, E)$ where V represents the vertices (variables)

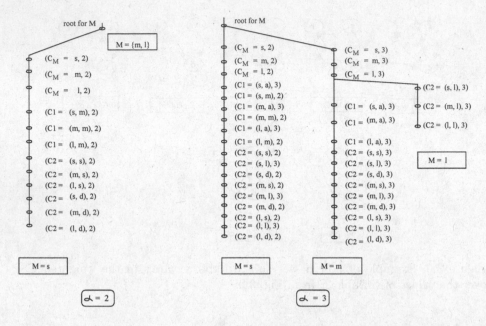

Figure 3.7: Example of a search of α–interchangeability computing by the use of discrimination trees.

(with $n := |V|$) and E edges (constraints) (with $e := |E|$); the density is computed as $denscsp = \frac{e - e\_min}{e\_max - e\_min}$, where $e\_min = n - 1$ and $e\_max = \frac{n(n-1)}{2}$;

- *Problem tightness:* This measure is obtained as the average of tightness of all the constraints. Since we will consider in the following fuzzy *CSPs* and weighted *CSPs* mapped on the interval $[0, 1]$, we compute tightness as the ratio between the sum of the semiring values associated to all the tuples in all the constraints, and the number of all possible tuple. A different, less precise but more general, way to compute tightness in Soft *CSPs* have been used in [78] as the ratio among the number of tuple with assigned semiring level greater than **0** and the number of all possible tuples.

3.6.1 $\delta/\alpha NI$

For both fuzzy and weighted *CSPs* we observed that the density and number of variables do not influence too much the occurrence of interchangeable values. There is instead a (weak) dependency from the domain size: *the number of interchangeable values increases with the resources.* This result from the test is obvious when dealing with crisp *CSPs*, but for soft problems this could be not so obvious.

We followed the model of measuring *NI* sets developed in [25] with some adaptation needed in order to deal with soft constraints. We report here the re-

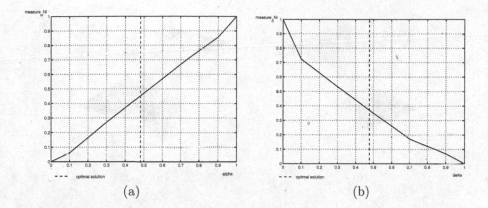

(a)   (b)

Figure 3.8: A statistical measure the number of NI of α interchangeability for Fuzzy CSP (with uniform weight distribution), for sets of problems with 10 variables and 10 values domains, on the left side of the figure, varying with α and similarly for δ.

sults for problem sizes n = 10 and n = 20, while varying the density $dens - csp \in \{0.1, 0.2, \ldots, 1\}$ and the maximum domain size $dom - size = \{\frac{n}{10}, \frac{2n}{10}, \ldots, \frac{9n}{10}, n\}$. For each case, 10 random problems were generated and then graphically represented by considering the measures described below.

In all the graphs we highlight where is the position of the optimal solution. In fact, when dealing with crisp $CSPs$ there is not any notion of optimality, but for soft $CSPs$ each solution has an associated level of preference. It is important to study NI occurrence around optimal solutions because we are often interested to discard solutions of bad quality.

Fuzzy CSP

Informally, for fuzzy $CSPs$ the weights assigned to the tuples represents how much the tuple is satisfied. The semiring operations are for combination the min and for projection the max.

Let us define $measure_\alpha NI$ as the 'occurrence' of NI $_\alpha$interchangeable value pairs. It computes the average number of $_\alpha NI$ interchangeable pairs values over the whole CSP divided by the potential number of relations using the formula:

$$measure_\alpha NI = \frac{\sum_{k=1}^{n} \frac{\alpha NIV_k*2}{domSize_{V_k}*(domSize_{V_k}-1)}}{n},$$

where n represents the problem size and $_\alpha NI$ V_k all the $_\alpha$interchangeable pairs values for variable V_k.

In Figure 3.8, we represent $measure_\alpha NI$, thus as said before the NI occurrence, for different values of α. It has been notice that around optimal solution

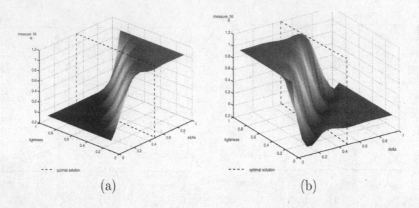

(a)   (b)

Figure 3.9: A statistical measure the number of α interchangeability for Fuzzy *CSP* (with uniform weight distribution), for sets of problems with 10 variables and 10 values domains, on the left side of the figure, varying with α and problem tightness, similarly for δ.

the number of $_\alpha$interchangeable values is high and it decreases with α. During the experiments, it has been noticed a weak dependence on the density of the *CSP* and that $_\alpha NI$ interchangeable values that increases with the number of resources.

Let us define $measure_\delta \mathrm{NI}$ as the 'occurrence' of NI $^\delta$interchangeable value pairs. It computes the average number of $_\delta \mathrm{NI}$ interchangeable value pairs over the whole *CSP* divided by the potential number of relations using the formula:

$$measure_\delta NI = \frac{\sum_{k=1}^{n} \frac{\delta NIV_k * 2}{domSize_{V_k} * (domSize_{V_k} - 1)}}{n},$$

where n represents the problem size and $^\delta NIV_k$ all the $^\delta$interchangeable pairs values for variable V_k.

In Figure 3.8, we see that around the optimal solution the occurrence of $^\delta NI$ interchangeable values do not depend on δ which varies around the optimal solution. It depends as in α case slightly on the density of the *CSP* and increases as well with the number of resources.

In Figure 3.9, we represent how the occurrence of $(^\delta/_\alpha)$interchangeability depends on α and δ, respectively and also on the problem tightness.

As we can see in the Figure 3.9, the number of α interchangeable values depend on α, but also on the problem tightness. For low tightness, the number increases faster with the values of α, while for higher values of tightness interchangeable values appear only for high values of alpha.

On the right side of the Figure 3.9, we have the dependence on δ and problem tightness. There, interchangeable values occurrence increases fast with the tightness for low δ values, while for high delta values it appears only for high tightness.

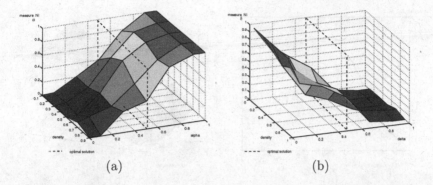

(a) (b)

Figure 3.10: A statistical measure the number of α interchangeability for Fuzzy *CSP* (with uniform weight distribution), for sets of problems with 10 variables and 10 values domains, on the left side of the figure, varying with α and problem density, similarly for δ.

In the Figure 3.10, we represent how the occurrence of $({}^{\delta}/_{\alpha})$interchangeability depends on α and δ, respectively and also on the problem density. We can notice that the interchangeability occurrence does not vary with the problem density and it varies in the same way with α and δ as before.

Weighted *CSPs*

In the following we present how the occurrence of ${}^{\delta}$ neighborhood interchangeable values varies with δ. The tests are not done for α as well as the semiring of weighted *CSPs* is not idempotent and thus ${}_{\alpha}$ neighborhood interchangeable values cannot be computed.

In Figure 3.11 (a), we see how the number of ${}^{\delta}$ neighborhood interchangeable increases with δ and that around optimal solution approaches to 1. This means that all the values pairs are interchangeable for high δ.

In Figure 3.11 (b), we represent how the measure of NI varies with δ and the *CSP* density as well. We can see as in the fuzzy case that the *CSP* density does not influence the occurrence of interchangeability.

3.6.2 NI versus FI

Computing full interchangeable values might be a quite costly operation as it may require computing all the solutions. There are not known efficient algorithms which can compute in polynomial time full interchangeable values. A localized but stronger condition than full interchangeability, called neighborhood interchangeability, can be computed in polynomial time.

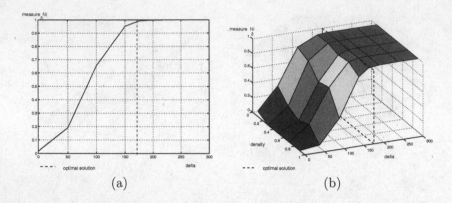

(a)   (b)

Figure 3.11: (a) The figure represents how δ NI values are varying with δ, for weighted $CSPs$ (b) The figure represents how δNI values are varying w.r.t. δ and the CSP density, for weighted $CSPs$.

Fuzzy CSP

We proposed in [9, 10] an extension of the algorithm introduced by Freuder [42] able to compute neighborhood interchangeability for soft $CSPs$. We also extended to soft $CSPs$ the property that $^\delta/_\alpha NI$ approximate $^\delta/_\alpha FI$.

Since NI is a subset of FI, it is important to know the ratio between the number of neighborhood interchangeable values and the number of full interchangeable values.

We consider in the tests randomly generated problems of size 10 with maximum domain size of 10 values at different densities, following the same model as described above.

We present here only the results for $^\delta NI$ interchangeability,

$$ratioNIFI = \frac{\sum_{k=1}^{n} \delta NIV_k}{\sum_{k=1}^{n} \delta FIV_k},$$

where $^\delta NIV_k$ represents the number of $^\delta NI$ interchangeable values pairs for variable V_k and $^\delta FIV_k$ represents the number of $^\delta FI$ interchangeable values pairs for variable V_k.

In Figures 3.12 we see that the ratio is between 0.7 and 0.9 around optimal solution for fuzzy CSP. Thus, NI interchangeability can well approximate FI interchangeability.

Weighted $CSPs$

In Figure 3.13 (a) we can see how the number of $^\delta$ neighborhood interchangeable values versus $^\delta$ full interchangeable varies with δ. The number of interchangeable values found by applying the neighborhood interchangeability definition is close

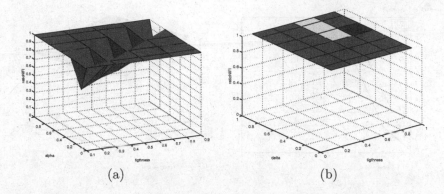

(a)   (b)

Figure 3.12: The ratio between the number of α neighborhood interchangeable values and α full interchangeable and its dependence on α, on the left side of the picture, for problems of 10 variables with 10 values domains and various values for density and tightness; similarly, we study the behavior for δ, on the right side of the figure.(a) Fuzzy $CSPs$ versus α. (b) Fuzzy CSP versus δ.

to full interchangeability values number. Thus, we can again approximate full interchangeability with neighborhood algorithm.

Using the same procedure as in Fuzzy $CSPs$ we computed the occurrence of neighborhood interchangeability relative to full interchangeability on randomly generated problems of size 10 with maximum domain size of 10 values at different densities, following the same model as described above.

We present here only the results for $^{\delta}NI$ interchangeability.

$$ratioNIFI = \frac{\sum_{k=1}^{n} \delta NIV_k}{\sum_{k=1}^{n} \delta FIV_k},$$

where $^{\delta}NIV_k$ represents the number of $^{\delta}NI$ interchangeable values pairs for variable V_k and $^{\delta}FIV_k$ represents the number of $^{\delta}FI$ interchangeable values pairs for variable V_k.

In Figure 3.13 (b), we represent how the ratio between $^{\delta}NI$ and $^{\delta}FI$ varies with delta and CSP density. We can see that the ratio is between 0.8 and 1 and this lead us to the conclusion that neighborhood interchangeability can approximate fairly full interchangeability for weighted CSP when we allow a solution degradation with δ.

3.6.3 NI versus Approximated NI Computed by the DT Algorithm (Only for Fuzzy $CSPs$)

When the times is idempotent we can use the DT algorithm to compute an approximation of the interchangeability. In this section we compare the number of

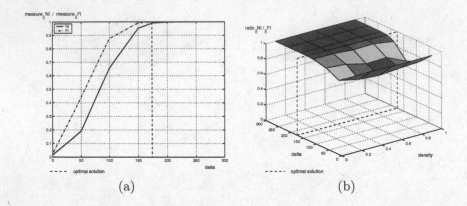

(a)   (b)

Figure 3.13: (a) The figure represents how $\delta\ NI$ versus $\delta\ FI$ values are varying with δ for weighted *CSPs*. (b) The figure represents how ratio $\delta\ NI/\ \delta\ FI$ is varying with δ and *CSP* density for weighted *CSPs*.

interchangeability in a Fuzzy *CSP*, with the amount of interchangeable values computed by the *DT* algorithm.

In Figure 3.14, we can see in the left side of the figure how the number of $_\alpha$ full interchangeable values, $_\alpha$ neighborhood interchangeable computed using the definition algorithm and discrimination tree algorithm respectively are varying with the values of alpha. We can see that the general algorithm for computing $_\alpha$ neighborhood interchangeable finds a close number of interchangeable values to full interchangeable ones.

The Discrimination Tree algorithm finds also a close number of interchangeable values to ones found by the definition algorithm.

For $^\delta$ interchangeability we can see the results in the right side of the Figure 3.14. We can see that the graphs almost overlaps. Thus the number of interchangeability values found for $^\delta$ neighbourhood/full interchangeability is almost the same. Thus, in δ case our method approximates even more full interchangeability.

Following these results we can get to conclusion that full interchangeability in fuzzy *CSPs* can be well approximates by neighborhood approximation based on the definition algorithm and the Discrimination Tree algorithm respectively.

3.7   Partial Interchangeability

As defined in 2.3.2, partial interchangeability is a weaker form of interchangeability then full and respectively neighborhood interchangeability. Thus, two values of a *CSP* variable are *partial interchangeable* when by interchanging them some variables might differ but the rest of the *CSP* is not affected.

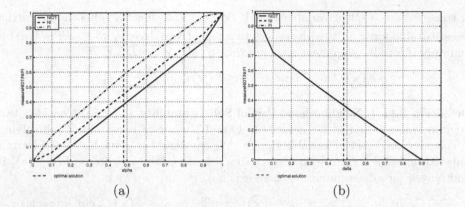

(a)   (b)

Figure 3.14: The figure represents how $\alpha\ NI$, $\alpha\ FI$, $\alpha\ NIDT$ values are varying with α, on the left side of the figure. The same for δ in the right side.

In this section we define this form of partial interchangeability and give algorithms for computing it. Further, we had explored its occurrence depending on the CSP parameters and the allowed threshold, α, of degradation, δ.

3.7.1 Definitions

Similar to Freuder [42] we define here some notions of substitutability/interchangeability that consider more than one variable and that extend our previous work in [9, 10]. In the following definitions we admit to change the value of the variable v together with some other neighborhood variables to obtain a notion of *Full Partial Substitutability (FPS)*.

Definition 3.9 (Full Partial Substitutability (FPS)) Consider two domain values b and a, for a variable v, and the set of constraint C; consider also a set of variable $V_1 \in V$. We say that b is *partially* substitutable for a on v with respect to a set of variables V_1 ($b \in FPS_v^{V_1}(a)$) if and only if for all assignment η there exists $\eta', \eta'' : V_1 \to D$ s.t.

$$\bigotimes C\eta[\eta'][v := a] \leq_s \bigotimes C\eta[\eta''][v := b]$$

Similarly all the notion of $^\delta/_{\alpha/\alpha-\text{set}}$Neighborhood Partial Substitutability ($^\delta/_{\alpha/\alpha-\text{set}}NPS$) and of $^\delta/_{\alpha/\alpha-\text{set}}$Full/Neighborhood Partial Interchangeability ($^\delta/_{\alpha/\alpha-\text{set}}FPI/NPI$) can be defined (just considering the relation in both directions and changing C with C_v).

Definition 3.10 ($^\delta$Neighborhood Partial Substitutability ($^\delta NPS$)) Consider two domain values b and a, for a variable v, and the set of constraint C_v involving

v; consider also a set of variable $V_1 \in V$. We say that b is $^\delta$Neighborhood Partial Substitutable for a on v with respect to a set of variables V_1 ($b \in {}^\delta FPS_v^{V_1}(a)$) if and only if for all assignment η there exists $\eta', \eta'' : V_1 \to D$ s.t.

$$\bigotimes C_v \eta[\eta'][v := a] \times \delta \leq_S \bigotimes C_v \eta[\eta''][v := b]$$

Definition 3.11 ($_\alpha$Neighborhood Partial Substitutability ($_\alpha NPS$)) Consider two domain values b and a, for a variable v, and the set of constraint C_v involving v; consider also a set of variable $V_1 \in V$. We say that b is $_\alpha$Neighborhood Partial Substitutable for a on v with respect to a set of variables V_1 ($b \in {}_\alpha FPS_v^{V_1}(a)$) if and only if for all assignment η there exists $\eta', \eta'' : V_1 \to D$ s.t.

$$\bigotimes C_v \eta[\eta'][v := a] \geq_S \alpha \implies \left(\bigotimes C_v \eta[\eta'][v := a] \leq_S \bigotimes C_v \eta[\eta''][v := b] \right)$$

Definition 3.12 ($_{\alpha-set}$Neighborhood Partial Substitutability ($_{\alpha-set}NPS$)) Consider two domain values b and a, for a variable v, and the set of constraint C; consider also a set of variable $V_1 \in V$. We say that b is $_{\alpha-set}$Neighborhood Partial Substitutable for a on v with respect to a set of variables V_1 ($b \in {}_{\alpha-set} FPS_v^{V_1}(a)$) if and only if for all assignment η there exists $\eta', \eta'' : V_1 \to D$ s.t.

$$\bigotimes C_v \eta[\eta'][v := a] \geq_S \alpha \implies \bigotimes C_v \eta[\eta''][v := b] \geq_S \alpha$$

Let's apply the definition of *NPI* to our running example in Fig. 3.1 in Section 3.2, by projecting over variable x. It is easy to see that a and c are Neighborhood Partial Interchangeable. In fact they have assigned both the semiring level 0.2. We have also that a, b and c are $_{0.15}NPI$ and $_{0.1-set}NPI$.

The next theorem shows how *NI* is related to *NPI*. As we can imagine, interchangeability implies partial interchangeability.

Theorem 3.12
Consider two domain values b and a, for a variable v, and the set of constraint C involving v; consider also a set of variable $V_1 \in V$ and its complement $\bar{V}_1 = V - V_1$. Then,

$$NI_v(a/b) \implies NPI_v^{V_1}(a/b).$$

Proof. It is enough to show that $b \in NS_v(a) \implies b \in NPI_v^{V_1}(a)$ (the results for interchangeability easily follows from substitutability). By definition

$$b \in NS_v(a) \iff \bigotimes C_v \eta[v := a] \geq_S \bigotimes C_v \eta[v := b].$$

It is enough to take $\eta' = \eta'' = \emptyset$, to easily have

$$\bigotimes C\eta[\eta'][v := a] \leq_S \bigotimes C\eta[\eta''][v := b]. \qquad \square$$

Similar results follow for the degradation and the threshold notion of partial interchangeability.

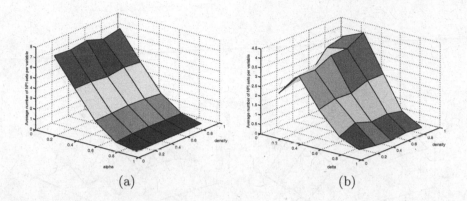

Figure 3.15: The figure represents how average number of NPI sets per variable is varying with α, figure (a), respectively δ, figure (b) and CSP density in Fuzzy $CSPs$.

3.7.2   Estimation of NPI occurrence

Further, we make experiments in order to estimate the occurrence of partial interchangeability in soft $CSPs$.

The following results were obtained on random generated Fuzzy $CSPs$, containing 10 variables and with domain sizes of 5 values. We consider a random CSP tightness and we are concerned by now only how the occurrence of partial interchangeability varies with the density of the CSP and either with the allowed threshold, α or degradation, δ.

The experiments were conducted in the following way. For each density in the set $\{0.1, 0.3, \ldots, 0.9\}$, we vary either α or δ between 0.1 and 0.9 and generate 20 random problem. For every values pair of each variable we compute if NPI set is existent.

In Figure 3.15, we represent how the average number of NPI sets per variable varies with the CSP density and with the threshold α, Figure 3.15 (a), or degradation δ, Figure 3.15 (b).

We can see that the number of the occurrence of NPI sets depends insignificantly on the density but varies strongly with the threshold or degradation. We remark that contrary to NI values the average number of NPI sets depends in the same way on α and δ. While, for high threshold/degradation, meaning small values of α/δ, we have high occurrence up to 4.5 average number of NPI sets per variable; this occurrence decreases for low threshold/degradation, high values of α/δ.

Next, we had measured the average size of the NPI set depending on the same parameters. As in Figure 3.16, we see that the average size stays between 0.5 and 3 number of variables in a NPI set. While decreasing with high values of the threshold α the size of NPI set does not depend much on the degradation δ,

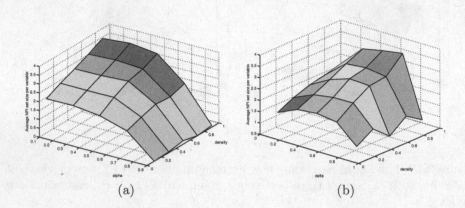

Figure 3.16: The figure represents how the average size of *NPI* set is varying with α, figure (a), respectively δ, figure (b) and *CSP* density for Fuzzy CSPs.

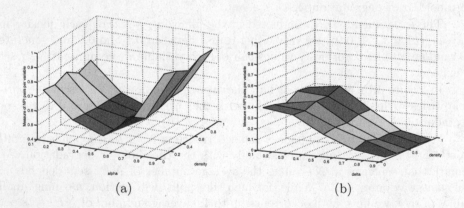

Figure 3.17: The figure represents how the average size of *NPI* set is varying with α, figure (a), respectively δ, figure (b) and *CSP* density for Fuzzy *CSPs*.

see Figure 3.16 (a) and (b) respectively. It increases with the CSP density.

In Figure 3.17, we measure the average number of NPI values pairs per variable normalized to the variable domain size. We can see that the number of NPI pairs do not depend on the density, but increases with the threshold α and decreases with degradation δ. We found that there are more values NPI $_\alpha$interchangeable then $^\delta$interchangeable.

3.8 Conclusion

Interchangeability in $CSPs$ has found many applications for problem abstraction and solution adaptation. We have shown how the concept can be extended to soft $CSPs$ in a way that maintains the attractive properties already known for hard constraints.

The two parameters α and δ allow us to express a wide range of practical situations. The threshold α is used to eliminate distinctions that would not interest us anyway, while the allowed degradation δ specifies how precisely we want to optimize our solution. We have shown a range of useful properties of these interchangeability concepts that should be useful for applying them in similar ways as interchangeability for hard constraints.

In fact, interchangeability may be practically more useful for soft constraints as it could be used to reduce the complexity of an optimization problem, which is often much harder to solve than a crisp constraint satisfaction problem. Furthermore, in the case of soft interchangeability it is possible to tune the parameters α and δ to create the levels of interchangeability that are required for the desired application.

Chapter 4

Multi Agent Computation of Interchangeability in Distributed $CSPs$

4.1 Introduction

Many distributed problems and applications such as planning, scheduling, resource allocation, configuration, etc., can be represented as distributed constraint satisfaction problems, in which the variables and constraints are distributed among distinct communicating agents. In this case, distribution of computation (in the form of distinct software agents) is adopted as a means to engineer a solution in a more effective way, and agents are usually assumed to be *cooperative*.

In this chapter we argue that interchangeability can be computed in non centralized/distributed environments, namely *Distributed Constraint Satisfaction Problems* based on collaborative multi agents systems. We show that multiple agents can collaborate to solve neighborhood and partial interchangeability in distributed constraint satisfaction problems.

When the CSP problem knowledge is distributed among multiple agents, there are few aspects which need to be considered: how computation tasks can be usefully divided among agents, how each agent can exploit the information provided by the other agents and how the agents can communicate in an effective way. All these issues are addressed in this chapter as follows.

4.2 Background

Due to advances in hardware and networking technologies, information is often decentralized and spread in different locations. Multi agent systems prove to be an appropriate framework in the development of parallelism in computation because of their intrinsic distributed nature and the distribution of processes and tasks among agents. In such systems, a number of agents share the work required to solve computational problems.

There are multiple problem classes in AI that have been addressed by search algorithms computed by collaborative multiple agents and one of them are the constraint satisfaction problems. Cooperative distributed solving is an AI domain for which a general framework was proposed by Lesser in [60], and is concerned with how a set of artificial intelligent agents collaborate and work together to solve problems.

Many AI problems as planning, scheduling, resource allocation, configuration, etc., for which constraint satisfaction problems modeling proved to be appropriate, are naturally distributed or were originally centralized but distribution is expected to help with their resolution. All of these problems have a distributed representation based on distributed constraint satisfaction problems ($DCSPs$) as showed in [52], [72] and [109]. A formalization of the $DCSPs$ framework and a survey on its algorithms were given by Yokoo and Durfee in [105].

Further, applications of multi agent systems where agents collaborate for distributed problem solving arise in fields such as sensor networks [67] [73], distributed and reconfigurable robots [85], multi agent teamwork [89], resource allocation [46] and human–agent organizations [23].

There is significant work in distributed constraint satisfaction for formalization and search algorithms ([109], [110], [86]). A *Distributed Constraint Satisfaction Problem* ($DCSP$) is defined/formalized as a constraint satisfaction problem in which variables and constraints are distributed among multiple agents [107].

There are two main groups of algorithms proposed this far in distributed constraint satisfaction problems: search algorithms and consistency algorithms. Besides consistency and search algorithms, in this work we study search algorithms for value symmetries, so called interchangeable.

In the following, we give an overview of the algorithms proposed for solving $DCSPs$.

The straightforward and trivial, but wasteful and unpractical, algorithm for solving $DCSPs$ is the centralized backtracking. The main idea of the algorithm is to select a leader agent which collects all the information about the variables, their domains and constraints, from all the other agents and then performs the solving of the CSP with standard centralized $CSPs$ methods. This algorithm is not feasible because of communication overhead between agents, wasteful because it does not take advantage of the parallelism as only the leader agent performs the computation and sometimes also not possible due to data privacy which involved agents might request.

To overcome the centralization of this computation the *synchronous backtracking* algorithm has been proposed. The algorithm assumes that the agents will make an agreement on the order in which they contribute to solving the CSP. The algorithm works as follows: each agent receives a partial solution from the previous agents and instantiates its variables such as to resolve its constraints in terms of variables held by previous agents. If the agent cannot locate satisfying values for its variables, it sends backtrack messages to the previous agents. Otherwise the search passes the partial solution onto other agents. This solution for solving *DCSPs* reduces the communication overhead, but it does not take advantage of distribution as only one agent at a time is performing calculations. A variation of synchronous backtracking, called *network consistency protocol*, was proposed in [30]. In this algorithm the agents construct a depth–first search tree and act synchronously by passing the computation right. In this case agents with the same parent in the tree can act concurrently.

Further studies have found algorithms which reduce the communication overhead and take advantage of agent parallelism. For reaching these goals the computation has to be asynchronous. For *asynchronous backtracking (ABT)* some solutions have been proposed by the research community. In [105], an asynchronous backtracking algorithm is proposed. In this algorithm agents run concurrently and asynchronously gaining computation time and power over the synchronous algorithms. So, there are two types of agents: value sending agents and constraint evaluating agents. Each agent instantiates its variable and communicates the variable value to relevant agents. The agents are linked in a directed way, where one of the two agents involved in the constraint/link is assigned that constraint, and receives the other agent value. The agents instantiate their values concurrently and send their values to agents which are connected by outgoing links. The constraint evaluation agents receive values of the value agents and verify satisfiability of the constraints. If the constraints are not satisfied they send backtracking messages to value agents. In [105], it is proven that this algorithm is sound and complete.

Asynchronous backtracking algorithm considers the case where access to variables is restricted to certain agents but constraints may have to be revealed. A different approach regarding privacy is proposed in [86], [87], where constraints are private but variables can be manipulated by any agent. This algorithm is called *asynchronous aggregation search* and it differs from previous approach in that it treats sets of partial solutions, i.e., every agent owns multiple variables that it assigns values to, and exchanged information concerns aggregated valuations for combinations of variables, instead of constraints. The *asynchronous weak commitment (AWT)* algorithm is a variation of *ABT* algorithm and proposes distributed search methods based on the min–conflicts algorithm [80]: a partial solution is not modified, but completely abandoned after a failure [104]. The *AWT* algorithm is complete if all no–good messages are maintained and it is about 10 times faster than the *ABT* approach. However, the explosion of no–good messages is the most difficult part to control. To coordinate the different forms of asynchronous interactions, the algorithms establish a static or a dynamic order among agents that determines the cooperation patterns between agents. Nishibe et al. [71] discuss and evaluate asynchronous backtracking with different ordering schemes: value ordering, variable ordering and value/variable ordering. In particular, they apply these techniques to the communication path assignment in communication networks.

Other algorithms inspired from centralized $CSPs$ have been further adapted for distributed environments such as: distributed consistency algorithm in [109], distributed breakout algorithm for $DCSPs$ in [108] and distributed partial constraint satisfaction in [52].

When CSP problems have to model not only dependencies between variables values but also preferences, cost or probabilities over variables values assignments, we deal with constraint problems optimization. These problems proved to need specific algorithms for their resolution which take into consideration the preference, cost or probability optimization. A straightforward extension of asynchronous backtracking algorithm to distributed constraint optimization problems ($DCOPs$), was proposed in [51] and relies on converting an optimization problem into a sequence of $DCSPs$ using iterative thresholds. But this algorithm applies only to limited types of optimization problems and has failed to apply to more general $DCOPs$ and even rather natural ones as minimizing the total number of constraint violations ($MaxCSPs$). Another synchronous solution has been proposed in [52]. As it requires synchronous, sequential communication it tends to be too slow. Other fast, asynchronous solutions, based on local search have been proposed in [52] and [110], but they cannot provide guarantees on the quality of solution. A polynomial–space algorithm for $DCOP$ named *Adopt* is guaranteed to find the globally optimal solution while allowing agents to execute asynchronously and in parallel, see [67].

4.3   Interchangeability in Distributed $CSPs$

In this section, we propose polynomial algorithms for computing different forms of interchangeability in a distributed environment.

In the first part we describe the distributed CSP formalism we have used, next we present a distributed algorithm for neighborhood interchangeability, namely *distributed neighborhood interchangeability*. Further, we give algorithms for computing partial interchangeability, which we formally call *distributed neighborhood partial interchangeability*.

4.3.1   Distributed $CSPs$ definitions

A distributed CSP is a constraint satisfaction problem (CSP) in which variables and constraints are distributed among multiple automated agents. The aim is to find a consistent assignment of values to variables which satisfy all the constraints and are allowed by the agents.

Distributed $CSPs$

In a distributed CSP all the information about the problem, i.e. variables, values and constraints, is distributed among agents. We consider the same $DCSP$

formalism as in [107]. Therefore we make the following assumptions about the communication properties between collaborative agents:

- Agents communicate through messages. An agent can send messages to other agent iff it knows its address.

- The delay in delivering a message is finite and for the transmission between any pair of agents, messages are received in the order they were sent.

A generic model would be that each agent has some variables and tries to determine their values by satisfying the constraints between them. On the other hand, there are constraints between agents, interagent constraints, and the value assignment must satisfy these constraints as well. Thus, the agents have to establish the values that their variables take by exchanging messages and agreeing with the other agents. We recall the CSP formalism can be expressed as: n variables $x_1, x_2, \ldots, x_n$, whose values are taken from finite, discrete domains $D_1, D_2, \ldots, D_n$, respectively, and a set of constraints on their values which here are expressed as predicates $p_k(x_{k1}, \ldots, x_{kj})$. Formally there exists m agents and each variable x_j belongs to one agent i: this relation is represented as $belongs(x_j, i)$, see [107]. Constraints are distributed among agents as well. The fact that agent l knows a constraint predicate p_k is represented as $known(p_k, l)$. As in [107], the $DCSP$ is solved iff the following condition is satisfied:

- $\forall$ i, $\forall$ x_j where $belongs(x_j, i)$, the value of x_j is assigned to d_j, and $\forall$ l, $\forall$ p_k where $known(p_k, l)$, p_k is true under the assignment $x_j = d_j$.

In our study, we make the following assumptions.

- Each agent has exactly one variable.

- All constraints are binary.

- Each agent knows all constraints relevant to its variable.

We believe that these assumptions are without loss of generality as they can be relaxed in a straightforward manner to general cases, where multiple variables are assigned to one agent and constraints are not only binary.

In the algorithms description we use the same identifier x_i for the agent and its variable.

4.3.2 Neighborhood Interchangeability Algorithm

The centralized algorithm for computing neighborhood interchangeable values was proposed by Freuder in [41], see Chapter 2, Section 2.2. This is a constructive algorithm and is computable in polynomial time. In the following, we propose the computation of this algorithm in a distributed environment.

Our algorithm takes advantage of the distributed environment and distributes the computational effort among the neighbor agents.

We consider a distributed CSP as described above, in which all constraints are binary, the variables are the nodes and constraints are the links between the nodes. Since each agent has exactly one variable, a node is also an agent.

We consider two types of agents: the *critical* agent who wants to interchange its values and its *neighbor* agents to which the critical agent is connected by constraints.

Definition 4.1 (Simplified Discrimination Tree) A *simplified DT* is a DT where we consider in the branches only the assignments of a restricted number of neighboring variables but not all.

The simplified DT is constructed in neighbor agents for the values to interchange received from the critical agent and relative to their own variables.

The *distributed neighborhood algorithm* contains the following steps:

1. the critical agent sends messages to all its neighbor agents with the two values he wants to interchange.

2. each neighbor agent confirms upon reception and then computes a *simplified discrimination tree* for the values to interchange with the critical agent.

3. the neighbor agents send messages to the critical agent with the results obtained in the simplified DT they constructed. These messages specify if the values to interchange with the critical agent are in the same branch annotation or they reach different branch annotations.

4. the critical agent analyzes the answers received from neighbor agents and if for all neighbor agents the interchangeable values are in the annotation of the same branch then they are interchangeable. Otherwise, if for at least one neighbor agent the values are not in the same branch annotation they are not interchangeable.

The algorithm can be straightforwardly extended to receive as input a subdomain of values of the critical variable instead pairs of values to be interchanged.

We consider two kind of messages for the communication between the cooperative agents:

- $REQUEST_1$ message – the critical agent sends messages of type REQUEST to all its neighbor agents. The message contains the two values to interchange, i.e. '$NI_{Interchangeable} \ x_{i1} \ x_{i2}$?'.

- $INFORM$ messages –

  - the neighbor agents first confirm reception of the request by the use of an $INFORM_1$ message.

  - then, each of them computes the simplified DT for the received values to interchange from the critical agent and answer with messages of $INFORM_2$ type. The messages are of two types: '$NI_{Interchangeable} \ x_{i1}$

x_{i2} YES' when the values are at the end of the same branch, meaning NI relatively to the current neighbor assignments, or '$NI_{Interchangeable}$ x_{i1} x_{i2} NO' when they are not.

In the following we give the procedures for the critical agent:
procedure $send_{NI}(NI_{interch}?, X_i, x_{i1}, x_{i2})$
1: **for** each neighboring agent X_j **do**
2:     send $REQUEST_1$ message $NI_{interch}?$ for values x_{i1}, x_{i2}
procedure $check_{NI}(x_{i1}, x_{i2})$
1: **if** $INFORM_2$ is a $YES_{interch}$ for all neighboring agents **then**
2:     return x_{i1}, x_{i2} are NI.
3: **else**
4:     return x_{i1}, x_{i2} are not NI.

The neighbor agents are responding based on the following procedures:
procedure $received_{NI}(NI_{interch}?, X_i, x_{i1}, x_{i2})$
1: send $INFORM_1$ to X_i received $NI_{interch}?, X_i, x_{i1}, x_{i2}$
2: interch $= simplified_{DT}(X_i, x_{i1}, x_{i2})$
3: **if** interch $=$ true **then**
4:     send $INFORM_2$ $YES_{interch}$ to the critical agent
5: **else**
6:     send $INFORM_2$ $NO_{interch}$ to the critical agent
procedure $simplified_{DT}(X_i, x_{i1}, x_{i2})$
1: **for** each value v $\in \{x_{i1}, x_{i2}\}$ **do**
2:     **for** each value x_j of variable X_j consistent with v **do**
3:         **if** $\exists$ a child node $X_j = x_j$ **then**
4:             Move to it
5:         **else**
6:             Create node $X_j = x_j$.

All the experimental tests are made on a JADE multi–agents platform [4]. Each time an agent wants to know if two of its values are interchangeable, it will send a $REQUEST_1$ message to its neighbors, by **procedure** $send_{NI}$. For example, in the Figure 4.1, we have a CSP with mutual constraints distributed among agents, where each variable is maintained by one agent and each agent knows the constraints associated to its variable. Agent X_2 wants to know if its values v and w are interchangeable. Thus, it sends a message : '$NI_{interchangeable}$ v w ?', to its neighbors X_1 and X_3. The neighbors confirm the request, by **procedure** $received_{NI}$, and start computation of the simplified DT algorithm, **procedure** $simplified_{DT}$. After the computation they will send an $INFORM_2$ message with the result: if the two values reach the same DT annotation the neighbor agent will answer 'YES', otherwise 'NO'.

The critical agent, X_2 in our example (see Figure 4.1) collects all the answers from the neighbor agents and decides if the two values v and w are interchangeable, by **procedure** $check_{NI}$. If all the answers are 'YES' then the two values are

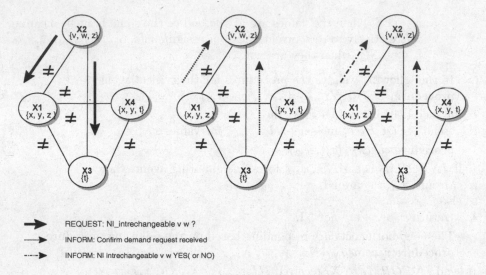

→ REQUEST: NI_intrechangeable v w ?

⋯▶ INFORM: Confirm demand request received

⋯▶ INFORM: NI intrechangeable v w YES(or NO)

Figure 4.1: An Example of Neighborhood Interchangeability Algorithm in *DCSPs*.

interchangeable, and if at least one answer is 'NO' they are not.

Soundness, completeness and complexity

In the following we discuss the soundness, completeness and complexity of Distributed NI algorithm.

Theorem 4.1

Distributed NI is sound: if it returns a pair of values I then this pair is NI for the critical variable.

Distributed NI is also complete: if the set I is NI for critical variable X_i, then it will find it.

Proof. We show that the distributed Neighborhood Interchangeability algorithm always determines if the values are interchangeable or not. According to the neighborhood interchangeability algorithm presented in Section 2.2, two values are NI if they reach the same annotation in the Discrimination Tree. In the distributed NI algorithm, the computation of the DT is distributed among agents, but the unification of the answers in critical agents implies identical results, annotation as in a centralized discrimination tree. Thus, as the distributed NI algorithm returns the same results as its centralized version, it is sound.

Furthermore, based on the assumption that all the messages between agents are always received and that unification of answers in the critical agent gives the same results as in centralized version, the distributed NI algorithm always finds the result (interchangeable or not) and thus, is complete.   □

Complexity

The complexity of the algorithm as in Freuder [41] is $O(n^2 d^2)$, where n is the number of the CSP variables and d the maximal domain size. When the algorithm computes all the NI interchangeable values for the whole CSP and all possible value pairs to interchange the complexity is $O(n^2 \cdot d^3)$, where n is the number of CSP variables and d the maximum size of their domain. When the computation purpose is limited to a specific variable and its values to interchange pair of values of a certain variable which one might want to interchange, the complexity for the worst case is to $O(n \cdot d)$.

4.3.3 Minimal Dependent Set Algorithm

In this section, we study algorithms for computing weaker forms of interchange-ability, partial interchangeability, in distributed $CSPs$. As described in Chapter 2, Section 2.2, partial interchangeability captures the idea that values for a set of vari-ables may change among themselves, but be fully interchangeable with respect to the rest of the world.

We have developed algorithms for computing a minimal partial interchange-able sets, which we called minimal dependent sets (MDS), see Chapter 2, Sec-tion 2.5.1. Here, we present an algorithm for computing minimal dependent sets in a $DCSP$.

We consider the $DCSP$ formalism as described in the previous section where each variable is contained in one agent. We name the agent that contains the *critical* variable, *critical agent*. The critical agent initiates and coordinates the search for the minimal dependent set of values to interchange, the *interchangeable set*. The algorithm can be straightforwardly generalized for a subdomain of values to interchange of the critical variable domain, and furthermore for a set of variables with their corresponding interchangeable sets.

The *distributed minimal dependent set* algorithm is an incremental algorithm; it includes gradually in the *dependent set*, the neighbor agents for which the values to interchange are not in the same branch annotation. At the initial step the dependent set contains only the critical variable. The main steps of the algorithm are:

1. The critical agent sends messages to the neighbor agents with the values it wants to interchange (a pair or a subdomain).

2. The neighbor agents confirm upon reception and compute the simplified dis-crimination trees for the values to interchange of the critical variable relative to variables they contain.

3. The critical agent collects the answers from the neighbor agents. If for all the neighbor agents the values to interchange are in the same branch annotation in their simplified discrimination trees then the values are neighborhood in-

terchangeable. Otherwise, the critical agent includes in the dependent set all the neighbors for which the values are not in the same annotation.

4. The algorithm restarts based on the same concept: the critical agent sends messages to the neighbor agents of the obtained dependent set S. It iterates gradually in the same manner until all the simplified DTs of the neighbor agents contain in the critical annotation values from all variables of the dependent set.

As described below, the first 3 steps of the algorithm are the same as in the distributed neighborhood interchangeability algorithm. For their computation, we use the same messages as described in the previous section. If the change propagates further as in Step 4, we need to use messages which transmit also the domains partitions of variables in the set S which reach the critical annotation in the simplified DT computations.

Thus, in computing the minimal dependent set algorithm in $DCSPs$, besides $REQUEST_1$, $INFORM_1$ and $INFORM_2$ messages we need also the following messages for inter agent communication:

- $REQUEST_2$ message – the critical agent sends messages of type $REQUEST_2$ to all neighboring agents of dependent set S. The message contains the two values to interchange and the dependent set S, i.e. 'Compute DT x_{i1} x_{i2} S', compute simplified DT for values x_{i1}, x_{i2}, and the dependent set S.

- $INFORM_3$ message – each neighbor agent sends a message with the values of the variables from the set S which reach the annotation of its Simplified Discrimination Tree.

Briefly, the MDS algorithm works as follows: The critical agent initiates the computation of a minimal dependent set by asking all its neighbors if the values in the interchangeable set I of its variable are neighborhood interchangeable. The neighbors for which the answer is NO are inserted in a dependent set S together with the critical variable.

The computation continues in the same way for the obtained dependent set S. The critical agent sends request messages to the neighbors of set S. But for this type of communication, the critical agent needs to transmit to the neighboring agents the dependent set S for which computation is requested. Thus it uses the message type $REQUEST_2$ by the use of procedure $send_{DependentSet}$, described below. Each neighbor agent computes its simplified discrimination tree for the dependent set S and informs back the critical agent about the domain partitions obtained in the critical annotation for each variable in the set S. The critical agent decides using procedure $check_{MinimalDependentSet}$ and based on the answers received from the neighbor agents, if the current set S is a MDS set or to continue further search.

In the following we describe the two procedures which the critical agent needs for the computation of Minimal Dependent Set (MDS).

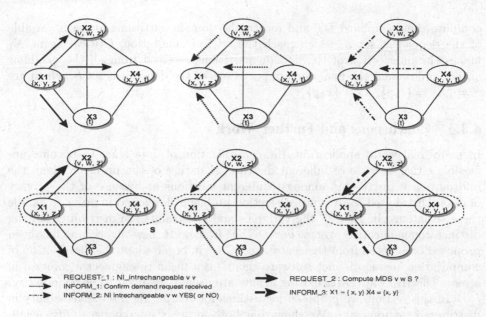

REQUEST_1 : NI_intrechangeable v v
INFORM_1: Confirm demand request received
INFORM_2: NI intrechangeable v w YES(or NO)

REQUEST_2 : Compute MDS v w S ?
INFORM_3: X1 = { x, y} X4 = {x, y}

Figure 4.2: An Example of computing Minimal Dependent Set(MDS) in a $DCSP$.

      procedure $send_{DependentSet}(X_i, x_{i1}, x_{i2}, S)$
1: **for** each neighboring agent X_j of S **do**
2:   send $REQUEST_2$ message $ComputeDependentSet$ for values x_{i1}, x_{i2}.

      procedure $check_{MinimalDependentSet}(X_i, x_{i1}, x_{i2}, S)$
1: collect the $INFORM_3$ answers from the neighboring.
2: **for** to each neighboring agent X_j of S **do**
3:   **if** $\exists$ an empty value set for one of the variables from the dependent set in the neighboring agents answer **then**
4:      include the corresponding agent in the new dependent set.
5:      Iterate = true.
6:   **if** Iterate **then**
7:      Restart the computation from step for the new dependent set.
8:   **else**
9:      A minimal dependent set is found. Return S.
10: Return dependent set S.

    In the Figure 4.2, we give an example of computing minimal dependent set in $DCSPs$. The critical agent X_1, sends $REQUEST_1$ messages to all its neighbors to demand if its values x and y are NI. Each neighbor agent computes the simplified DT. The neighbor X_4 replies NO. Further search is proceed for the dependent set $S = \{X_1, X_4\}$. The critical agent X_1 reiterates the computation and sends request messages to the neighbors of set S, X_2 and X_3 . Neighbors X_2 and X_3, compute their simplified DT and return the domain partitions for each variable of the dependent set S, which reach the critical annotation. Critical agent X_1 makes the intersection of the domain partitions received from all the neighbor agents and obtains the final domain partitions of the dependent set S, which are $S = \{X_1 = \{x, y\}, X_4 = \{x, y\}\}$.

4.3.4   Conclusions and Further Work

In many real–world application, the centralization of data start to become unfeasible either because of inherent distributed nature of the problem where the information is distributed amongst different locations or because of the privacy of data. Distributed constraint satisfaction problems developed in order to handle these situations. In $DCSP$, the variables and constraints are distributed among distinct communicative agents. For $DCSP$ framework new algorithms has been proposed or adapted from the centralized CSP in order adopt the distribution of computation among distinct software agents as a mean to engineer a solution in a more effective way. Participating agents are usually assumed to be cooperative.

In this section, we proposed algorithms for computing interchangeability in distributed environments. We show that both forms of interchangeability, neighborhood or partial, expressed through minimal dependent sets, can be computed also in distributed environments.

The proposed algorithms concern various aspects of distributed CSP computation as follows: the allocation of tasks amongst the agents, the exploitation of information generated by the other agents in each of the agents and the efficient communication among agents. The main goal of these algorithms is to propose solution adaptation variants where as the changes are localized to one CSP variable by distributed neighborhood interchangeability algorithms or to a set of CSP variables by minimal dependent set algorithm for $DCSPs$. Interchangeability methods have been proved to improved search in centralized $CSPs$. Specific search algorithms have been proposed to solve $DCSP$ since their distributed characteristic could not be handled by the centralized search algorithms. An important aspect of further research is to evaluate how interchangeability methods can improve search algorithms also in $DCSPs$. Some results regarding this aspect has already been given by Petcu and Faltings in [73] where they show that the performance of the distributed breakout algorithm can be improved using neighborhood interchangeability.

In further work the algorithm for computing minimum dependent set should be also adapted to distributed computation. This can be done in a straightforward manner following the same procedure as for minimal dependent set algorithm. Also some experimental evaluation concerning the algorithms efficiency and the number of exchanged messages between the agents on practical or random problems should be conducted.

Chapter 5

Interchangeability in Dynamic Environments

This part of our work studies how the algorithms for computing interchangeability can be adapted to dynamic environments.

5.1 Motivation

Many techniques were developed to deal with static $CSPs$, but many reasoning problems need to be solved in dynamic environments.

For example, in many practical applications the knowledge in the agent environment might change and evolve in time. As the knowledge in the environment changes, the agent plans for achieving its goals might have to change according to the last events. Thus, the agent has to adjust and adapt its plans according to the new changes. In static environments this situation is hard to handle since all the information about the problem to solve has to be known before the computation. We consider the domain of knowledge which can be represented as constraint satisfaction. Moreover, we consider that the knowledge about the problem is evolving in time and we represent this as dynamic $CSPs$.

Moreover, much of the work for computing dynamic constraint satisfaction problems ($DynCSP$) deals with searching of solutions, but there is less work in solution update for $DynCSPs$. Our work is motivated by the fact that once a solution of the CSP has been computed, one should not spare effort to recompute the solutions for the transformed CSP, which changed dynamically i.e. by a constraint relaxation or restriction, but to reuse those already computed for the previous CSP. On the already known solutions we can apply solution update techniques based on interchangeability.

Solutions for previous CSP might be computed in systematic way, or local search and also by applying solutions update techniques with interchangeability.

We will store the previous experience in terms of known solutions or interchangeability computations. In the case that we have to recompute, update solutions in the modified $CSPs$, we can update the old solutions by applying interchangeability algorithms accordingly to the new modified constraints. A faster way to compute solutions for the transformed CSP is to consider directly the data structures which compute interchangeable values for previous $CSPs$; and modifying them by considering the new constraints we can update the solutions of the old CSP and thus, find solutions for the transformed one.

5.2   Related Work

The concept of $DynCSP$ [33] has been introduced to handle situations where the CSP may evolve. In crisp $CSPs$, solving techniques make the assumption that the set of variables, their domains of values and the constraints between them are static and completely known before that the search begins. In real life problems, not always all knowledge about the problem can be known during the first phase of the problem solving. Moreover, in real life applications the environment might evolve, for example the set of tasks to be performed and/or their execution conditions might change, or the user requirements might evolve or change as well, for example in design, planning or scheduling. For handling these situations, there is a need for specific techniques adapted to solve the $DynCSPs$ in order to avoid to restart the entire solving process from the beginning any time a new changes appears.

As observed in previous research works, see [33] and [6], the changes in a $DynCSP$ are usually *gradual*. The changes to the problem knowledge are evolving slowly whereas the new changes are affecting only a small part of the problem but not the whole. We take for example a transport scheduling problem. There is need to configure a good schedule for truck drivers, clients and receivers. There are constraints over clients time windows, staff and trucks availability, trucks capacity and transportation costs. All these factors come into play when the transport logistic company starts its operation. However, every year there are often new staff and/or new trucks added to the traffic. These changes are all minor and it is obvious that having new staff should not have much effect on the order allocations to the trucks.

Due to this gradual characteristic of the $DynCSPs$, it is expected that there are similarities between the CSP solutions. The changes of the solution are localized to a set of variables in the CSP without affecting the entire problem. Some classification among the $DynCSP$ solutions has been done by Elfe in [19] in the domain of telecommunication services configuration. The differences between successive assignments are characterized by costs. Elfe propose a technique which can find a solution satisfying the new environment with minimum implementation cost.

There are three main sets of approaches that address $DynCSP$ problems:

- **Arc Consistency (AC)** – focuses on adopting arc–consistency techniques from static to $DynCSP$ as proposed by Verfaillie et al in [91] and Bessière in [6]. The arc–consistency algorithms proposed for static are not appropriate in dynamic environments. For example for constraints relaxations they are not able to determine the set of values that must be restored in the domain. This means that each time a constraint is added of removed from the CSP, all the variables need to be reset to their full domains and arc–consistency has to be applied from scratch. Much research has been done in order to adapt to $DynCSPs$ methods proposed for solving static $CSPs$. As $CSPs$ are NP problems, a special attention was accorded to filtering methods such as arc consistency which can remove local inconsistencies and thus, can reduce $CSPs$ problem search space. In [6], Bessière proposed algorithms for solving arc–consistency in $DynCSPs$, which are named (Dynamic AC–4). These algorithms uses counters which are keeping truck of the number of consistencies a value of a variable x_i has in other variable x_j. The values for which the counters are 0, are removed from the domain and all the other counters are iteratively updated.

The algorithm consists of two approaches:

- for a constraint restriction the computation of the counters is initiated meaning that whenever there are counters with value 0, their respective values are removed from the domain and all the other counters have to be updated recursively;

- for a constraint relaxation, a method for counter computation is proposed. This method is similar to the procedure for constraint restriction whereas the counters are incremented instead to be decremented whenever a constraint is relaxed.

Improved variants of this algorithm has been further proposed by Bessière in [7] and by Debruyne in [32].

- **Constraint recording method** – offers techniques that allows a $DynCSP$ to remember what has been discovered previously and use this knowledge to discover assignments that satisfy the new constraint set.

In [90], van Hentenryck et al. propose methods for maintaining a solution of the $DynCSP$ once that the current solution is not valid anymore since a new constraint is introduced. Inspired by this work, Schiex [84] proposed for the first time the idea of recording previous searches in terms of no good sets and introduced an algorithm to enhance search methods for $DynCSPs$ by solution maintenance approach. This algorithm uses prediction techniques which can foresee whether adding or removing a constraint is changing the part of the space that has already been checked. Furthermore, in [91], Verfaillie and Schiex are developing this methods and propose algorithms for solution reuse in $DynCSPs$. They propose methods for finding new solutions by producing local changes in already known ones.

In [35], Richards improved Schiex work based on no–goods search in *DynCSPs*. A method for classifying no goods is proposed. This methods can distinguish which which no goods are relevant for a specific search whereas the two sets of learning are distinguish among: *shallow learning* and *deep learning*.

- **Local search** – Other techniques for solving *DynCSP* use local search methods such as those proposed in [80], [77], [66]. Local repair methods consider some assignment and repair it using a sequence of local modifications. Unfortunately, there is no guarantee that they will find the nearest solution. In fact, Local Search may also wander off in the wrong direction, but many of the algorithms for Local Search do not benefit from constraint propagation to reduce the size of the search process. In [77], Roos et al. propose a local search algorithm based on arc–consistency algorithm. Some local search techniques have been applied also for soft constraints as in [66]. Miguel et al. propose algorithms for solving fuzzy *CSPs* in dynamic environments based on local search methods and k–consistency techniques.

In [44], Freuder and Wallace propose techniques for solving constraint satisfaction problems partially, in particular by satisfying a maximum number of constraints. These techniques could be also considered to be adapted for solving *CSPs* in dynamic environments.

A detailed survey of the related work on *DynCSPs* has been given by Bastani in [3].

5.3 Definitions

We consider as model for *DynCSP* the one defined by Bessière in [6].

Definition 5.1 (Dynamic *CSP* (*DynCSP*)) [Bessière 1991] A *dynamic* constraint satisfaction problem (*DynCSP*) $\wp$ is defined as a sequence of static *CSPs* $\wp_{(0)}$, $\ldots$, $\wp_{(\alpha)}$, $\wp_{(\alpha+1)}$, $\ldots$, each resulting from a change in the preceding one.

The change can be a constraint restriction or relaxation defined as follows:

Definition 5.2 (Constraint Restriction) [Bessière 1991] A *constraint restriction* is a new constraint imposed on the *CSP*. If we have $\wp_{(\alpha)} = (X, dom, \tau_{(\alpha)}, R)$, we will have $\wp_{(\alpha+1)} = (X, dom, \tau_{(\alpha+1)})$, where $\tau_{(\alpha+1)} = \tau_\alpha + 1$.

Definition 5.3 (Constraint Relaxation) [Bessière 1991] A *constraint relaxation* is a constraint removed from the *CSP*. So, a *CSP* $\wp_{(\alpha)} = (X, dom, \tau_{(\alpha)}, R)$ transforms in have $\wp_{(\alpha+1)} = (X, dom, \tau_{(\alpha+1)})$, where $\tau_{(\alpha+1)} = \tau_\alpha - 1$.

5.4 Algorithms

We now try to optimize the effort in computing interchangeable values in a $DynCSP$. As interchangeable values might have had been computed in a previous CSP to the current one, we try to reduce the computation of the interchangeable values of the current CSP by considering previous gained knowledge about how values interchange in the previous $CSPs$.

As it was proven in [2] that k–ary constraints can always be expressed as binary, we consider though our work only problems with binary constraints.

For simplification we assume that we have computed all the interchangeable values for all variables in each CSP in the sequence. For a new CSP in the sequence, we do not have to compute the DT tree structure from scratch, but just to modify the old ones from the previous CSP in the sequence.

In a second approach, we consider that not every variable of each CSP in the sequence has had it's interchangeable values computed. When we have a new CSP in the sequence and an interchangeability computation demand for one of its variables, we look for the closest CSP in the sequence which has the interchangeability values computed for the corresponding variable. The two $CSPs$ might differ with a number of constraints between 0 and the distance between them.

5.4.1 NI Algorithm for Constraint Restriction

Constraint restriction in a CSP considers imposing a new constraint. Imposing a new constraint in a binary CSP affects 2 variables of the current CSP [1]. So we have to reconsider the computation of the interchangeable values involved by the new constraint.

Constraint restriction prevents the occurrence of neighborhood interchangeability but might induce partial interchangeability. Choueiry et al. [25] and Benson and Freuder [5] find that there is high occurrence of neighborhood interchangeability up to a CSP density of 0.4. In Chapter 2, Section 2.5.1 we show that for high CSP densities there is high occurrence of partial interchangeability.

Constraint restriction in a $DynCSP$ holds the following property:

Property 5.1
Constraint restriction on a CSP $\wp_{(\alpha)}$, discriminates among the domains of values of the variables involved in the constraint in the new $\wp_{(\alpha+1)}$ and thus reduces the occurrence of neighborhood interchangeability.

So, $\forall d'_k \in NI'(X_i), \exists d_k \in NI(X_i)$, such that $d'_k \subseteq d_k$, where NI represents the set of neighborhood interchangeable values for variable X_i in $\wp_{(\alpha)}$ and NI', the same, for variable X_i but in $\wp_{(\alpha+1)}$.

---

[1] In the case of a k–ary constraint, k variables are affected be a constraint restriction and for which we have to recompute the interchangeable values.

For computation of the neighborhood interchangeable values of affected variables by the constraint restricted in $\wp_{(\alpha+1)}$ there is no need for the entire DT structure computed in the context of the precedent CSP $\wp_{(\alpha)}$, but only its annotations, thus the neighborhood interchangeable sets. As said before, we consider the framework of binary $CSPs$; so, only two variables of the CSP' need neighborhood interchangeability recomputation.

In the following, we present the algorithm which computes neighborhood interchangeable values when we have a constraint restriction. It applies for a variable X_i, where we denote as NI the sets of interchangeable values in $\wp_{(\alpha)}$ before restriction and as NI' the sets of interchangeable values in $\wp_{(\alpha+1)}$, after the restriction. Variable X_j is the variable imposed by the restricted constraint. For each domain partition $d_k \in NI$ we construct a DT tree relative to imposed variable X_j.

Algorithm 14: Algorithm to compute neighborhood interchangeability for constraint restriction in $DynCSPs$

Input: critical variable X_i, restricted variable X_j.

1:   $NI' \leftarrow \phi$
2:   **for all** $d_k \in NI$ **do**
3:     Create the root of the discrimination tree for current annotation d_k
4:     **for all** $v_i \in d_k$ **do**
5:       **for all** $v_j \in X_j$ **do**
6:         **if** $\exists$ child node $X_j = v_j$ **then**
7:          Move to it
8:         **else**
9:          Construct new node $X_j = v_j$
10:       Add $X_i = v_i$ to the one of the new annotations d'_k
11:       Go back to the root of the discrimination tree of d_k.
12:     NI' $\leftarrow$ include all d'_k
13:   return NI

Algorithm 14 can be straight forwardly extended for the k–ary constraints.

Algorithm 14 for constraint restriction can be extended in a straightforward manner to a set of constraint restrictions. If more variables then X_j are imposed to variable X_i we reconstruct the DT for each domain partition in former NI by considering all the new imposed variables.

We study further in Subsection 5.4.3, if constraint restriction can imply partial interchangeability.

5.4.2   NI Algorithm for Constraint Relaxation

Constraint relaxation has the reverse implications of constraint restriction. We show in the following that by relaxing a constraint in a CSP $\wp_{(\alpha)}$, the number of neighborhood interchangeable values either stays the same or increases. We express this more formally in the following property, observed also by Choueiry and Noubir in [28].

Property 5.2
Constraint relaxation of a CSP $\wp_{(\alpha)}$ to a new problem $\wp_{(\alpha+1)}$ can only increase the number of interchangeable values.

So, $\forall d_k \in NI(X_i)$, $\exists d'_k \in NI'(X_i)$ such that $d_k \subseteq dk'$.

For computing neighborhood interchangeable values for the new $\wp_{(\alpha+1)}$, we have either the simple choice to reconstruct the DT structures for the affected variables by the relaxation and thus, on a smaller neighborhood, or to modify the old DT structures of $\wp_{(\alpha)}$, if they where saved.

In the following we give the algorithms to recompute the old DT structure. As by constraint relaxation, the neighborhood is modified by reducing its size, we have to find algorithms which remove the nodes containing variables removed from the neighborhood.

Algorithm 15 works in the following way:

- we parse the DT tree in a depth first search manner, by using Algorithm 16;

- when a node contains variables relaxed by the constraint, thus removed from the neighborhood [2] we remove that node from the DT structure.

- the child nodes of the removed node have to be merged if they contain the same neighborhood variable having the same value, we call these *equal child nodes*.

- the merged child nodes are linked to the parent of the removed variable, see Algorithm 17.

- the algorithm stops when all the occurrences of the constraint relaxation variable are removed from the DT.

Algorithm 15: Algorithm to compute neighborhood interchangeability for constraint relaxation in $DynCSPs$
Input: critical variable X_i, relaxed variable X_k.

1: $X_p \leftarrow$ root of the DT(X_i).
2: **while** X_p not last DT node **do**
3:     procedure ParseDT(X_p, X_k).

Algorithm 15 for constraint relaxation can be extended in a straightforward manner to a set of constraint relaxations. Suppose that we have to compute the

---

[2]We remind here again that as we made the assumption that we work in the framework of binary constraints, only one variable has to be removed from the DT tree; also the algorithm is straightforward to extend for k–nary constraints.

NI values for variable X_i and that a set S_c of constraints have been relaxed in the CSP. We consider the set S_c of constraints which concern variable X_i directly and thus, the variables which linked before by those constraints to variable X_i have to be removed from the DT structure. Algorithm 15 can be easily modified to remove all the variables in the set S_c from the DT structure while parsing the DT.

These algorithms describe the computation for two consecutive $CSPs$ in the $DynCSPs$ sequence; they can be extended in a straightforward manner to reuse the NI values computation between more than 2 consecutive $CSPs$. Lets consider a CSP $\wp_{(\alpha)}$ and a CSP $\wp_{(\alpha+k)}$; they can differ with a maximum number k constraint restrictions or relaxations. For computing the NI values of variable X_i for the new CSP $\wp_{(\alpha+k)}$ we construct the set of variables which are relaxed, S_x, and the set of variables which are restricted, S_c relatively to CSP $\wp_{(\alpha)}$. Further we apply the algorithm for constraint relaxations for the set S_x and the algorithm for constraint restrictions for the set S_c and obtain the NI values for variable X_i in the new CSP $\wp_{(\alpha+k)}$.

Algorithm 16: procedure ParseDT(X_p, X_k)

1: **if** $X_p = X_k$ **then**
2:      remove X_p.
3:      foundVk = true.
4:      MergeEqualChilds(X_p).
5:      **for all** child X_p' of X_p **do**
6:         **if** X_p' is unvisited **then**
7:            **if** $X_p'\ ! = X_p$ and foundVk **then**
8:               Stop searching this branch.
9:            **else**
10:                 procedure ParseDT(X_p', X_k).
11:        Link the new merged child nodes to the parent of X_p.
12: **else**
13:     **for all** child X_p' of X_p **do**
14:        **if** X_p' is unvisited **then**
15:            procedure ParseDT(X_p', X_k)

Algorithm 17: MergeEqualChilds(X_p).

1: identify equal child nodes of X_p.
2: merge equal child nodes.
3: **for all** merged child mX_p **do**
4:     procedure MergeEqualChilds(mX_p).

In this section, we stated algorithms for the computation of neighborhood interchangeable values when a constraint is relaxed in the CSP. We need to have the DT structures of the previous $CSPs$ in which we remove the variables relaxed by the constraints.

5.4.3 MDS Algorithm for Constraint Restriction

In the following, we study how the MDS Algorithm, see Chapter 2, Section 2.5.1 can be optimized in dynamic environments when the MDS set was already computed in previous $CSPs$ of the $DynCSP$ sequence. We present the algorithm for recomputing the MDS set for two consecutive $CSPs$ in the sequence.

Property 5.3
Constraint restriction from a CSP $\wp_{(\alpha)}$ to a CSP $\wp_{(\alpha+1)}$ discriminate on the values of one variable in the MDS set or might imply the spread of the MDS set to set MDS'.

So, let $X_k \in MDS$ be the variable constraint to the new variable X_j imposed by the constraint restriction. Thus, $d'_k \subseteq d_k$ for variable X_k in MDS after the restriction if MDS does not spread; otherwise, $MDS \subset MDS'$.

Algorithm 18 for computing a minimal dependent set for a constraint restriction from a CSP $\wp_{(\alpha)}$ to a CSP $\wp_{(\alpha+1)}$ follows these steps:

- if the variable X_j imposed by the constraint restriction discriminates among the values to interchange of the critical variable, than variable X_j is included in the MDS set and search for the new spread MDS set is continued by Heuristic1 4 or Heuristic2 5, see Section 2.5.1;

- otherwise, X_j discriminates among the values of the domain partition d_k of variable $X_k \in MDS$ to which it has constraint. If there exists values $v_k \in d_k$ which satisfies the whole domain of X_j then MDS stays the minimal dependent set. In another case, the algorithm continues by Heuristic1 4 or Heuristic2 5, see Section 2.5.1, for the spread set $MDS + X_j$.

Like in dynamic NI computation, Algorithm 18 can be extended in a straightforward manner for a set of constraints restrictions. One have to check how they affect the interchangeable set of the critical variable or the domain partitions of the other variables in the MDS and to increase the MDS set in an incremental manner.

5.4.4 MDS Algorithm for Constraint Relaxation

Here we give an algorithm for recomputing the minimal dependent set (MDS) when a constraint is relaxed in the CSP.

Property 5.4
Constraint relaxation from a CSP $\wp_{(\alpha)}$ to a CSP $\wp_{(\alpha+1)}$ can increase the domain partition of one of the MDS variables or might even decrease the minimal set.

Algorithm 18: Algorithm to compute MDS set for a constraint restriction in $DynCSPs$
Input: critical variable X_c, restricted variable X_j.

1: **if** X_j constraint to the critical variable X_c **then**
2:    construct reduced $DT(X_c)$ relatively only to the neighborhood $N = \{X_j\}$.
3:    **if** values in the interchangeable set I of the critical variable do not reach the same annotation **then**
4:       $S_{MDS} \leftarrow S_{MDS} \cup \{X_j\}$.
5:       $MDS \leftarrow \text{Heuristic1}(S_{MDS}, X_c, I)$, see Algorithm 4.
6:    **else**
7:       $MDS \leftarrow MDS$.
8: **else**
9:    construct $DT(X_k)$ relatively only to the neighborhood $N = \{X_j\}$, where $X_k \in MDS$ has constraint with X_j.
10:    **if** $\exists$ values $v_k \in d_k$ of variable X_k compatible with the entire domain of the imposed variable X_j by the constraint restriction **then**
11:       $MDS \leftarrow MDS$ but with domain partition for X_k restricted to all values v_k.
12:    **else**
13:       $S_{MDS} \leftarrow S_{MDS} \cup \{X_j\}$.
14:       $MDS \leftarrow \text{Heuristic1}(S_{MDS}, X_c, I)$, see Algorithm 4.
15: **return** MDS.

So, let $X_k \in S_{MDS}$ be the variable which had a constraint relaxed to the variable X_j. Then, the domain partition d'_k in the new MDS is larger than the old partition d_k, $d_k \subseteq d'_k$ for variable X_k or $S'_{MDS} \subset S_{MDS}$, if X_k does not have any constraint in the neighborhood of S_{MDS} and $\exists$ domain partitions for any variable in S_{MDS} is compatible with the same values of X_k as well as the values to interchange of the critical variable. Note that an MDS is represented by the variables it contains and their domain partitions. We note that S_{MDS} is the set of variables in MDS, see MDS characteristics in Section 2.5.1.

Algorithm 19 computes the minimal dependent set after a constraint relaxation follows these steps:

- if the constraint relaxation concerns the critical variable, we compute the discrimination tree for the critical variable and its values to interchange considering the neighbors of the MDS less the relaxed constraint variable. If the values to interchange reach the same annotation, they become NI and the algorithm stops returning as MDS only the critical variable. Otherwise, the domain partitions for the rest of variables in the MDS set are recomputed relatively to the reduced neighborhood.

Algorithm 19: Algorithm to compute MDS set for a constraint relaxation in $DynCSPs$

Input: critical variable X_i, relaxed variable X_j.

1: **if** relaxed constraint is to the critical variable X_c from variable X_j **then**
2:     Construct $DT(X_c, \text{Neighbors}(X_c) \setminus X_j)$
3:     **if** values to interchange from I reach the same annotation **then**
4:         $S_{MDS} \leftarrow \{X_c\}$
5:     **else**
6:         $MDS \leftarrow$ critical annotation of the reduced $JDT(S_{MDS}, X_c, I)$ relatively to the neighborhood $N = N_{S_{MDS}} \setminus \{X_j\}$
7: **else**
8:     **if** X_k after the relaxation to X_j do not have any other constraint to the neighborhood of MDS **then**
9:         $A \leftarrow$ critical annotation of the reduced $JDT(S_{MDS} \setminus \{X_k\}, X_c, I)$ relatively to the neighborhood $N = \{X_k\}$
10:         **if** $\exists d'_p \forall X_p \in S_{MDS} \setminus \{X_k\}$ in A **then**
11:             return reduced $MDS \leftarrow A$
12:         **else**
13:             $MDS \leftarrow$ critical annotation of the reduced $JDT(S_{MDS}, X_c, I)$ relatively to the neighborhood $N = N_{S_{MDS}} \setminus \{X_j\}$
14:     **else**
15:         $MDS \leftarrow$ critical annotation of the reduced $JDT(S_{MDS}, X_c, I)$ relatively to the neighborhood $N = N_{S_{MDS}} \setminus \{X_j\}$
16: return MDS.

- when another variable than the critical one has a relaxed constraint, we recompute the domain partitions of all the other variables in the MDS relative to the reduced neighborhood. When, by constraint relaxation, the variable in MDS does not have any other constraint to the neighborhood of MDS, test if MDS stays minimal by removing the relaxed variable from the set.

Algorithm 19 can be straightforwardly extended for a set of constraint relaxations.

Also, as for neighborhood algorithm, Algorithm 19 can be easily adapted to a set of constraint restrictions and relaxations.

5.5 Conclusions and Further Work

Many real–world problems are dynamic: in planning, unforseen events may appear while a plan execution, in scheduling, changes to the problem may occur as the schedule is being executed, or in configuration, some components of the configuration which are missing might need to be replaced with equivalent ones.

DynCSP framework have been proposed to handle these kind of problems. Specific algorithms for solving *DynCSPs* has been proposed or adapted from their centralized version. In this chapter, we showed how algorithms for computing neighborhood interchangeability and neighborhood partial interchangeability can be adapted to dynamic constraint satisfaction problems solving.

Constraint restriction and constraint relaxation can cover the modeling of any possible change in a *DynCSP*. For each of these operations we proposed specific algorithms which can compute neighborhood interchangeable values. Further more, we show that algorithms for computing minimal dependent sets which characterize partial interchangeability in *CSPs* can be adapted in dynamic *CSPs* when a constraint is restricted or relaxed. All these algorithms can be extended in a straight forward manner for more simultaneous constraint restrictions or relaxations.

As by applying interchangeability algorithms we can compute how changes in some variables propagate in the *CSP* and localize them to the set of affected variables, the use of these algorithms in *DynCSP* is an appropriate and important approach. The complexity of this algorithms depend highly on the *CSP* problem structure as the experimental results described in Chapter 2, Section 2.5.1 has shown. According to these results, one might expect that in low dense *DynCSPs* the changes localize to one variable and thus neighborhood interchangeability algorithms for constraint restriction or relaxation need to be applied. For more dense *DynCSPs*, algorithms which computes minimal dependent sets of possible changes can be used. The number of possible alternatives are increasing with the number of resources/values in the variables domains.

It has been shown that interchangeability is improving search in static *CSPs*. In the future work and important aspect to be studied is how interchangeability can improve search in dynamic *CSPs*.

Moreover, an important issue to be studied in further work is a comparative study between different solving techniques for dynamic *CSPs* such as interchangeability methods, arc consistency, constraint recording methods or local search in order to establish their efficiency and completeness relatively to the problem structure.

Chapter 6

Generic Case Adaptation Framework

In this chapter, we present a generic framework for the case adaptation process in case based reasoning systems for which the knowledge domain can be represented as constraint satisfaction.

Agent logic can not always and/or not entirely be properly captured and expressed in terms of choice making, based on constraint satisfaction. For instance, when values assignment to variables are not necessarily known a priori, it may be more opportune to adopt other reasoning approaches, such as case–based reasoning techniques. Moreover, case–based reasoning offers a means of applying learning capabilities to agent reasoning.

6.1 Case Based Reasoning Context

Case–Based Reasoning (CBR) is a recent approach to problem solving and learning that has received a considerable amount of attention over the last few years.

The reliance on past experience, that is such an integral part of human problem solving has motivated the use of *CBR* techniques. A *CBR* system stores its past problem solving episodes as cases which later can be retrieved and used to help solve a new problem. *CBR* is based on two observations about the nature of the world: that the world is regular, and therefore similar problems have similar solutions, and that the types of problems encountered tend to recur.

Case–based reasoning is a problem solving paradigm that in many respects is fundamentally different from other major AI approaches. Instead of relying solely on general knowledge of a problem domain, or making associations along generalized relationships between problem descriptors and conclusions, *CBR* is able to utilize the specific knowledge of previously experienced, concrete problem situations (cases). Case–Based Reasoning techniques solve problems by reusing, adapting and combining earlier solutions [58]. CBR based reasoners are able to learn simply by storing cases. A new problem is solved by finding a similar past case, and reusing it in the new problem situation. A second important difference is that CBR also is an approach to incremental, sustained learning, since a new experience is retained each time a problem has been solved, making it immediately available for future problems.

In CBR terminology, a case usually denotes a problem situation. A previously experienced situation, which has been captured and learned in a way that it can be reused in the solving of future problems, is referred to as a past case, previous case, stored case, or retained case. Correspondingly, a new case or unsolved case is the description of a new problem to be solved. Case–based reasoning is – in effect – a cyclic and integrated process of solving a problem, learning from this experience, solving a new problem, etc, see references in [20], [88], [55].

Case representation focuses on what information is contained in a case. The general purpose of a case is to enable future resolution of a new problem that is similar in nature but different in context. The context of a case is characterized by case's indexes, which describe under what circumstances it is appropriate to retrieve a case. A new problem is solved by retrieving one or more previously experienced cases, reusing the case in one way or another, revising the solution based on a previous case, and retaining the new experience by incorporating it into the existing knowledge–base (case–base). For a given input problem the CBR cycle is carried out in a common set of steps (see Figure 6.1), regardless the domain of the application:

- retrieve – extract a case for a similar problem.

- reuse – evaluate how the case fits to the new situation.

- revise – adapt that problem to fit to the new situation requirements.

- retain – learn by remembering successes and failures as new cases.

This cycle is illustrated in Figure 6.1, see [1].

An initial description of a problem (top of Figure 6.1) defines a new case. This new case is used to RETRIEVE a case from the collection of previous cases. The retrieved case is combined with the new case – through REUSE – into a solved case, i.e. a proposed solution to the initial problem. Through the REVISE process this solution is tested for success, e.g. by being applied to the real–world environment or evaluated by a teacher, and repaired if failed. During RETAIN, useful experience is retained for future reuse, and the case base is updated by a new learned case, or by modification of some existing cases.

As indicated in Figure 6.1, general knowledge usually plays a part in this cycle, by supporting the CBR processes. This support may range from very weak (or none) to very strong, depending on the type of CBR method. By general knowledge we mean general domain–dependent knowledge, as opposed to specific knowledge embodied by cases. For example, in diagnosing a patient by retrieving

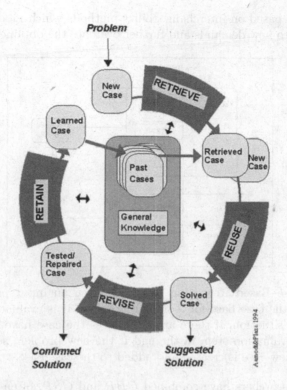

Figure 6.1: **Case–Based Reasoning Process**. The CBR Cycle

and reusing the case of a previous patient, a model of anatomy together with causal relationships between pathological states may constitute the general knowledge used by a CBR system. A set of rules may have the same role.

Based on the generic properties of Constraint Satisfaction Problems in modeling a wide range of problems, we propose here a framework model in CBR systems where the knowledge can be represented as $CSPs$. For this framework we propose generic adaptation methods based on interchangeability algorithms.

6.2 Framework Model

We have developed a framework for case–based reasoning (CBR) based on constraint satisfaction problems (CSP). As there are many generic techniques for indexing and retrieval in CBR systems but no general ones for adaptation, the main focus of our research is on case adaptation.

We consider a simpler CBR system as described in Figure 6.2. It consists of two main steps: one for retrieving and indexing cases which we call *recall*, and the *adaptation* step based on interchangeability methods which modify the retrieved case according to new demands and further evaluate the obtained case.

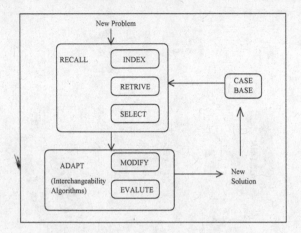

Figure 6.2: **Case–Based Reasoning Process**. Given an input problem a case is retrieved from the case base for a similar problem; it is evaluated how this case fits to the new situation, if there are differences the case have to be adapt and return to the evaluation step; in the end if the new problem solved brings new information a new case is created and added to the case base.

Several researchers have combined CBR and CSP, often with the goal of supporting the adaptation process. A good example is COMPOSER [75], a research prototype system aimed at exploring the use of CBR and CSP as applied to engineering design. In COMPOSER, the case–based reasoner was augmented with CSP techniques in order to achieve a more systematic adaptation process.

More similar to our approach is CADRE [54], a case–based reasoner for architectural design where constraints restrict numerical relationships among dimensions. CADRE introduced the concept of *dimensionality reduction*: before attempting to adapt a case, it constructs an explicit representation of the degrees of freedom available for adaptation. However, CADRE defined this approach only for numeric constraints.

The first approach of the framework presented here consists in a layered structure as shown in Figure 6.3.

The lowest level contains the CSP of the problem which represents the configuration. Based on the CSP network the interchangeable values are computed by determining the neighborhood interchangeable values of each variable and the partial interchangeable values for sets of variables.

The CBR layer uses the interchangeable values, precomputed in the interchangeable layer, in the adaptation step. The application interacts directly with the CBR level and with the interchangeability computation level for the adaptation phase.

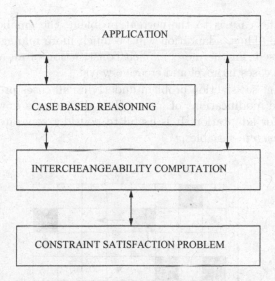

Figure 6.3: **Graphic representation of the framework**. The framework works based on a layered structure. The case adaptation is realized based on the interchangeability applied on the constraint satisfaction problem which model the problem to be solved (e.g. a configuration problem).

From the *CBR* perspective, constraint techniques are integrated in order to: formalize the ill–defined process of adaptation, enhance and make more rigorous case representation, develop a more systematic and/or efficient retrieval mechanism, provide a domain independent, general formalization, of representing a *CBR* task (e.g. retrieval, adaptation), make solutions easier to explore and help manage design preferences.

6.3   Case Adaptation by Interchangeability

This section describes the concept of adaptation(interpretation) of a case in a world model formulated as a *CSP* [68]. Assigning an interpretation to a case allows it to be adapted to a new situation while maintaining its correctness.

Many approaches to case adaptation have considered all elements of a case to be variable, thus making adaptation as complex as solving the problem from scratch. Our approach, already used very successfully in CADRE, is to consider adaptation as two steps:

1. construct a model of the case that contains only variables that are both relevant and modifiable, we call this *dimensionality reduction*.

2. search for an adaptation in this reduced model.

The closer the case is to the current problem, the smaller the model for adaptation will be. Thus, adaptation will be much more manageable than if the base model was used. Furthermore, explicit construction of an adaptation model allows us to reuse cases in novel and creative ways.

The constraint satisfaction problem underlying all cases provides the knowledge of admissible modifications of a case. The difficulty is how to exploit it to compute models for adaptation. It is useful to consider separate mechanisms for *continuous* and *discrete* variables.

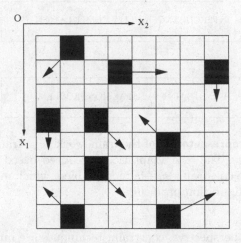

Figure 6.4: **Graphic representation of two dimensional discrete space**. Black squares represent solutions given as cases. By applying neighborhood interchangeability, we can find similar solutions which differ in only one dimension, shown graphically by horizontal or vertical arrows.

In the domain of discrete variables, the adaptation space is less obvious. In [99], Weigel, Faltings and Choueiry looked for interchangeability in subproblems induced from the original CSP by reducing the domains of a selected set of variables. Usually it is not possible to compute a single dimensionality reduction which is valid across the entire design space. We show how the concept of interchangeability allows us to nevertheless compute a dimensionality reduction for discrete variables.

The concept of Interchangeability formalizes equivalence relations among objects or between values in a CSP problem.

The adaptation model for a case thus consists of all variables which the customer might have to change, plus the interchangeability values which are applicable to the case and define what can be changed.

We take as the example a problem with two discrete variables X_1 and X_2 as in Figure 6.4. Black squares represent solutions given as cases. By applying neighborhood interchangeability, we can find similar solutions which differ in only one dimension, shown graphically by horizontal or vertical arrows.

However, this severely restricts the possibilities: we might also want to adapt along a diagonal direction. This requires *partial* interchangeability: changes to a variable value which also requires changes in another one.

Partial interchangeability can be considered as full/neighborhood interchangeability on a *set* of variables. Thus, it can be computed using the same algorithms. The difficulty, however, is to know what sets of variables to consider. In fact, the number of possibilities grows exponentially with the size of the considered sets, and a general search is clearly unmanageable.

A variable V affects the problem through the constraints that link V to other variables in the problem, thus through V's neighborhood $N(V)$. As observed in [28], if V is partially interchangeable with respect to S, then S must include at least one node of $N(V)$. Thus, it makes sense to compute partial interchangeability by considering increasingly large neighborhoods of V. In [41], Freuder gives an efficient algorithm for computing neighborhood interchangeability values in this context.

We will consider in the following a simple example of car configuration. The variables which describe the car and the constraints between them are shown in Figure 6.5.

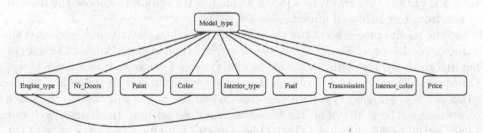

Figure 6.5: **Graph of the constraint network**. In the figure the squares represent the variables of the constraint satisfaction problem linked by constraints.

Returning to our application, a case is constructed by assigning one solution of the car configuration CSP to a well–defined buyer profile.

When a new buyer makes a request, the case database is browsed and the new buyer profile is matched to the closest one. The corresponding solution of the selected case is presented to the new buyer. For example, the system will have the following interchangeable values of the variables in the solution of the case 15 (see Table 6.1). Possible changes for the current solution are presented in terms of interchangeable values applied to the car configuration variables.

In Table 6.1 we present some results obtained for the constraint network considered in Figure 6.5. By applying the Neighborhood Interchangeability algorithm for each variable we will get the corresponding neighborhood interchangeable values. For example, for the variable Model–type, the values Opel–Tigra, Opel–Corsa

Attributes	Values	Neigh. Interch. Values	Partial Interch. Values
Model–type	Opel–Tigra	Opel–Corsa, Opel–Sintra	Opel–Omega/Engine–type Opel–Astra/Color
Engine–type	E–75HorseP	–	E–90HorseP/Model–type
Nr–Doors	3Doors	–	–
Paint	Metallic	–	–
Color	Beige	Prune, Blue–Ber, Rouge	Gris–Quarts/Model–type Blanc/Model–type Gris–London/Model–type
Interior–type	Standard	–	–
Transmission	Manual	–	–
Interior–color	Diasit–Rouge	Diasit–Blue, Houston–Blue Takana–Impala	–
Price	83000	–	–

Table 6.1: **Case 15 with interchangeability values**. This example shows the interchangeable values of the variables in the solution of the case 15.

and Opel–Sintra are neighborhood interchangeable; that means that all the solutions which contains one of these values will still remain solutions by exchanging with one of the other two values. So, a buyer has the option to choose the desired model from the displayed interchangeable values.

The results table also shows the partially interchangeable values obtained for variable Model–type. To obtain these values, we applied the Minimal Dependent Set algorithm for the critical variable Model–type and values to interchange Opel–Omega and Opel–Astra. We obtained knowledge that the change spreads to the MDS set $S = \{$Engine–type$\}$. In this case, when the buyer will change the value of a variable, the values of all the variables from the set have to change. So if our buyer would prefer the model Opel–Omega instead of Opel–Tigra the type of the engine will change.

6.4   Case Adaptation

Case–based reasoning (CBR) for solving problems can be broken down into two important steps: case *retrieval* and case *adaptation* [58]. While there are many general methods for case retrieval, case adaptation usually requires problem–specific knowledge and it is still an open problem. In this study, we propose a general method for solving case adaptation problems for the large class of problems which can be formulated as Constraint Satisfaction Problems($CSPs$). This method is based on the concept of *interchangeability* between values in problem solutions. The method is able to determine how change propagates in a solution set and generates a minimal set of choices which need to be changed to *adapt* an existing solution to a new problem based on the MDS Algorithm, see Chapter 2, Section 2.5.1.

Although it may be unrealistic to hope for generic methods to solve all adaptation problems, one class of problems which may be addressed is problems which can be formulated as $(CSPs)$. CSP problems are a generic paradigm and this makes them a valuable class of problems for CBR adaptation methods. Solutions which can be shown to apply to CSP type problems can be applied to a wide range of problems.

This research work presents a method based on the concepts of interchangeability [41] for realizing case adaptation.

6.5   Adaptation Model Based on Constraint Satisfaction

In a previous section we introduced case adaptation based on constraint satisfaction and gave a car configuration example.

In this section we present the design of the adaptation engine, where the domain knowledge models a resource allocation problem using $CSPs$, see [26].

We recall that the resource allocation problem can be defined as a CSP in the following way:

- tasks $(T_1, T_2, \ldots, T_n)$ are considered as the variables of the CSP where their values are resources.

- domains of variables are sets of resources by which the tasks can be executed.

- constraints among variables denote mutual exclusion with respect to the values. That means that two tasks overlapping in time cannot be carried out by the same resource.

Since the main contribution of this work relates to the adaptation step of the CBR process, retrieval is achieved using a simple metric which picks out the closest previous case.

6.5.1 CBR Model

The framework presented in Figure 6.6 solves new resource allocation problems by retrieving and adapting previous solutions. The problem solving process proceeds as follows:

1. A new problem (defined in terms of tasks and resources to allocate as above) arrives in the system.

2. The problem is matched to a single previous case.

3. The adaptation phase of the process therefore receives the following inputs:

   - The solution of the retrieved case.

   - The corresponding CSP retrieved from the CSP base according to the tasks contained in the new problem.

- The differences between the problem at hand and the one expressed in the indexing parameters of the retrieved case[1] (see Figure 6.6).

4. The adaptation module applies the minimal NPI algorithm (Section 2.6.2) to this input to generate the closest solution to the new problem.

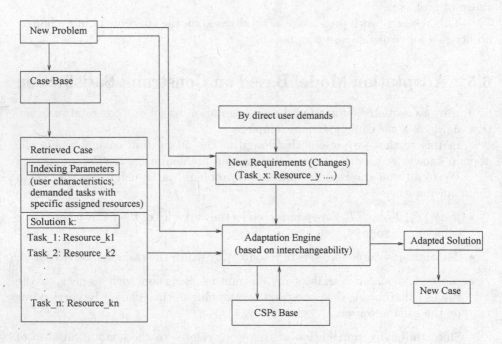

Figure 6.6: Adaptation Model

The adaptation phase of the process therefore has an extra form of information available to it which is the CSP model corresponding to the new problem. The domain knowledge is represented as a CSP problem. It is this that allows us to apply the interchangeability algorithms. Inferring a new solution from an already known one by studying local changes based on interchangeability, have a linear cost and can be used as a reliable adaptation method.

For the tasks with their corresponding exchanging values, provided by the new requirements module, the adaptation engine applies the minimal dependent set (MDS) algorithm, see Chapter 2, Section 2.5.1, in order to find the minimal set of changes for adapting solutions. For an input of a single task, it might find that the values proposed to be exchanged are NI, and thus the new solution keeps all the same values for all the other tasks and exchanges only the NI values of the task asked to be changed. In other cases the algorithm might find an MDS set of variables which have to be changed in order to get a solution for the new

---

[1]The requirements can also be imposed by the user.

requirements. Thus the constraints between the variables of the *MDS* set have to be solved, while all the others variables of the solution stay unchanged. We notice that the computational effort is here restricted to the *MDS* set and one does not have to solve the whole problem from scratch. If the *MDS* set finding algorithm does not find any *MDS* set, it means that there are no solutions for the new requirements in the limited threshold of number of variables which might be changed imposed in the *MDS* algorithm. In this situation, it might be necessary to solve the problem from scratch.

In the *CSP* base we store the knowledge about the domain in the form of *CSPs*. In the previous section, the car configuration system had only one *CSP* which modeled all possible configurations [68]. For increasing the generality, we now propose to represent the knowledge by several *CSPs*, which model different resource allocation problems.

6.5.2 Example of Applying Neighborhood Interchangeability (NI) to Case Adaptation

Using a resource allocation example we show how to use NI values and *NPI* values for solution adaptation. As shown in Chapter 6, we define a generic framework for the case adaptation process of case based reasoning systems for which the knowledge domain can be represented as a constraint satisfaction problem.

As presented in previous work, the simplest way to apply interchangeability to case adaption is to find NI sets of values for a variables of the *CSP*. Figure 6.7 shows an example of this for a resource allocation problem. It is inspired from Choueiry and Noubir [28]. The resource allocation problem is modeled as a discrete *CSP* in which the constraints are binary and denotes mutual exclusion with respect to the values. The nodes of the *CSP* represents the tasks to be executed, and their values are sets of resources by which these tasks can be executed. Arcs link tasks that overlap in time and have at least one resource in common.

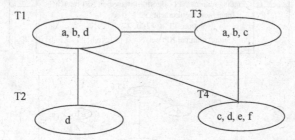

Figure 6.7: Simple example of how resource allocation is modeled as *CSP*

For example, in the *CBR* cycle a new problem might match a solution such as:

$$Sol_1 = \{T_1 = a, T_2 = d, T_3 = b, T_4 = e\},$$

but impose the new requirements to allocate resource f to task T_4. Normally this requirement could have a knock on effect on all or many other choices but in this case the values e and f of variable T_4 are NI. Thus the exchange does not affect the other variables and it stays a solution of the CSP (and hence a valid solution to the whole problem). Formulation of the problem as a CSP and applying the algorithm for detecting NI allows us to detect and prove this (which may be non–trivial in other representations).

6.5.3   Example of Applying Partial Interchangeability (PI) to Case Adaptation

Applying NI is useful but only allows single values to be exchanged in a solution. This makes a very strong requirement that zero other choices are impacted by changing an assignment. PI is a weaker form of NI and thus, more frequent in any given solution since several interdependent choices can be varied together while leaving the rest of the problem unchanged. The consequence is to isolate the effect of modification to a subproblem of the CSP. It identifies qualitatively equivalent solutions which can be generated by modifying the values of the indicated variables only.

Since PI is more frequent in a solution, it increases the flexibility and utility of the adaptation module. The example given in Figure 6.8 illustrates how the adaptation module works when using PI interchangeability on the example from Figure 6.7.

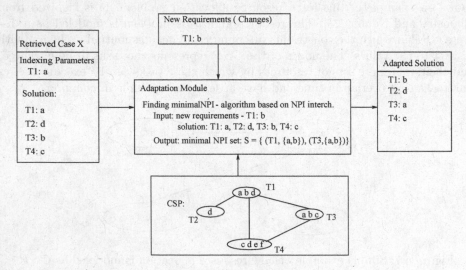

Figure 6.8: Adaptation engine based on crisp $CSPs$.

The Adaptation module receives as input the solution of the retrieved case, the CSP corresponding to the current solution and the requirements which it has to adapt according to the requirements from the user or not matching with the indexing parameters. Indexing parameters contain previous user requirements; in this example the requirements are the tasks with the corresponding resources. The similarity measure used in computing the closest case is only a matching procedure between the new requirements and the previous requirements which are now the indexing parameters of the case. The differences between requirements, i.e. $T_1 = a$ have to become $T_1 = b$, gives the input for the MDS algorithm, Chapter 2, Section 2.5.1, which computes the MDS set containing PI values.

As we can see in Figure 6.8, by 'adapting' the task T_1 from resource a to resource b we have to also change the task T_3 from resource b to resource a in order to keep a solution, while all the other tasks remain the same. Change across two variables is therefore detected while leaving the rest of the solution valid. The system also works when several changes are required at once by using an extended version of the MDS Algorithm as an input of several variables and their interchangeable sets.

Once the MDS sets have been identified, the adaptation module can check to see if it can find a valid solution that respects the changes imposed by the new problem w.r.t. the retrieved case.

6.6 Soft Constraint Satisfaction for Case Adaptation

In Section 6.5 and in [69], we proposed a generic framework for case adaptation for the domain of problems for which the knowledge domain can be represented as crisp *Constraint Satisfaction Problems (CSP)*.

The CSP model can be applied to a wide range of problems as diagnosis, planning, scheduling, robot control, and configuration but there are still many real–life problems which cannot be precisely defined by using crisp constraints only. Soft constraints allow the use of preference associated to either constraints, or variables, or tuples within the constraints. We propose adaptation methods for the domains of problems where the knowledge can be represented as a *Soft CSPs*. Certain domains must be represented as hard constraint satisfaction problems in order for the resulting solution to be functional. For example, in the configuration of a product, the components have to match so that the product is functional. However, many other real–life problems are more naturally handled by using soft constraints [82, 15].

In Chapter 3 and in [10], we defined two notions: *threshold* α and *degradation* δ for substitutability and interchangeability in Soft *CSPs*, called $((^\delta/_\alpha)substitutability/interchangeability)$. Fortunately, soft constraints also allow weaker forms of interchangeability where exchanging values may result in a degradation of solution quality by some measure δ. By allowing more degradation, it is possible to increase the amount of interchangeability in a problem to the desired level, and thus the possibilities for adapting solutions. $^\delta$substitutability/interchangeability is a concept which ensures this quality.

Ideally, one would like to compute values which are interchangeable over global solutions, i.e., *fully interchangeable*, but this is computationally expensive. In this way, the search of the values is computed in a local form, called *neighborhood interchangeability*. Just as for hard constraints, full interchangeability is hard to compute, but can be approximated by neighborhood interchangeability which can be computed efficiently and implies full interchangeability. We have defined the same concepts for soft constraints, and proven that neighborhood implies full $(\delta/_\alpha)$substitutability/interchangeability, see [9].

We propose here to apply these techniques in a CBR system where the knowledge domain is represented as a soft CSP. By allowing a certain degradation *delta* of a case or searching over a certain threshold *alpha* one can try to realize adaptation. So, we show how case adaptation can be realized based on these concepts.

The main contribution is a generic model for the application of soft interchangeability techniques to a large class of CBR adaptation problems (Section 6.6.2). We present an example of a sales manager system for car configuration domain (Section 6.6.1).

6.6.1   A CBR System for Product Configuration

We present here how the CBR system works for a configuration problem example. However, the framework works in the same manner for all the problems which can be represented as a CSP, i.e. as planning scheduling, diagnosis, etc.

We have applied and tested constraint satisfaction based methods in a case based reasoning system which function as a sales manager. The case base reasoning system contains cases which represent past sales and consist of a buyer profile and the chosen product. The configuration of the product is modeled as a constraint satisfaction problem. While admissible configurations can be precisely specified as a constraint satisfaction problem, each customer has particular needs that remain largely unformalized. Case–based reasoning maps properties of the customer to these implicit customer needs and product configuration that would fit these needs. Constraint satisfaction techniques can then be used to adapt the proposed solution by the CBR system to the particular customer requirements and preferences.

In Figure 6.9, we represent the general framework of our system. When a new customer makes a new demand, the sales system will search in the case base for similar cases using of buyer profile for case indexing and retrieval.

Each case contains:

- A buyer profile containing:

    - characteristics: e.g. age, family status, using purpose for the car, budget limits in the car investment,

    - particular preferences/requirements for the car.

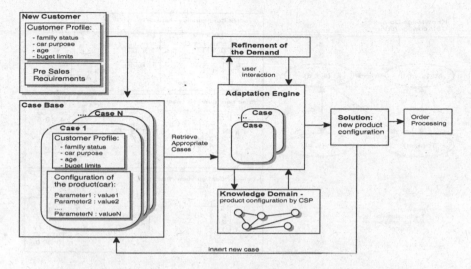

Figure 6.9: An electronic sales manager based on a CBR system.

- The chosen product contains the configuration of the car as a constraint satisfaction problem solution where each component of the car has assigned a value consistent with all the other components. The components are represented as variables of the CSP, according to the constraints between them.

The retrieved cases are sent to the adaptation engine which communicates with the buyer for further refinement of the demands. The adaptation engine uses interchangeability methods in order to adapt the solutions of the product configuration. The domain knowledge is represented as a constraint satisfaction problem. By interacting with these two modules the adaptation engine reaches the new solution which together with the current buyer profile is inserted in the case base. The sale order is then sent for processing.

In our example we present three models for representing the knowledge, as shown in Figure 6.10:

- The first example represents the configuration of the product modeled as a crisp CSP where the constraints are either satisfied or not by a tuple of values. In order that the product be functional all the components have to be compatible with one another.

- In the second example, we model the price configuration for the cost of the product as a weighted CSP. The weights on the tuples of values represent the cost for each component (by unary constraints) and the costs for combinations of components respectively (by binary constraints).

- The last example represents the delivery of the product modeled as a fuzzy CSP where the preferences on the tuples of values represent the delivery

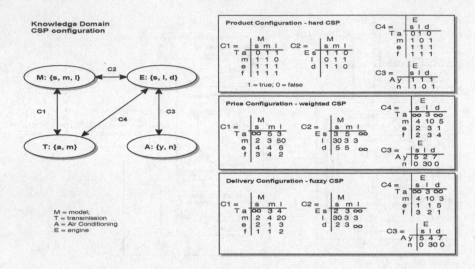

Figure 6.10: Domain knowledge as Constraint Satisfaction Problems.

time of the components and the combinations of components according to the constraints between them.

While the configuration of the product has to be expressed with crisp constraints such that the product to be feasible, modeling the price and delivery time with soft constraints allows for the use of customer preferences. The identified solutions are then ranked according to the optimization criteria used by the soft constraint system.

6.6.2   Adaptation Model with Soft Constraint Satisfaction

In Section 6.5, it is shown how the adaptation process is realized through the use of NI interchangeability and PI interchangeability characterized by MDS sets. Now, we propose adaptation for the problems which are represented as soft constraint satisfaction problems and we use $^{\delta}_{\alpha}$interchangeability to adapt solutions. In this model, the adaptation is realized by interchanging values of one or a subset of Soft CSP variables by allowing a certain degradation of the solution.

The adaptation model is illustrated here through an example application to a generic product configuration problem. The configuration of the product is defined as a CSP where:

- the components of the product are expressed as the variables of the CSP;

- the domains of the CSP are the sets of values that the components can take;

- the constraints among variables denote the dependency between the components in order that the product be functional.

In order to model this product configuration example, we have used two representative forms of Soft $CSPs$: the weighted one to model the price and the fuzzy one to model the delivery time. So, for modeling the price of the product, the modeling of the CSP is the same as for the crisp constraint case, only that we have cost for each value assignment of each component (unary constraint) and for each tuple combination over the constraints (binary constraint). By the use of the semiring operations for weighted CSP, $< \Re^+, min, +, +\infty, 0 >$, see Chapter 3, for constraint combination we will have to add the costs in order to obtain the final price.

For delivery time we have used the fuzzy CSP model, where the semiring is defined as $< \Re^+, min, max, +\infty, 0 >$ [2], see Chapter 3.

The Architecture of the Adaptation Framework

The architecture of the system is domain–independent; its domain knowledge comes from three external sources: a case library, domain knowledge represented as CSP and user requirements, see Figure 6.11. Our sales manager system (shown in Figure 6.9), finds the appropriate product for a new buyer by retrieving cases and adapting their product configurations according to the new requests. The main contribution of this work relates to the adaptation step of the CBR process. Retrieval is managed by using a comparison metric over the buyer profile relative to profiles contained in cases and picks out the closest previous cases.

As in Figure 6.11, the adaptation module receives the retrieved cases from the case base. The module interacts with the user for specific, personalized requirements and with the domain knowledge for making consistent adaptations.

The adaptation process proceeds as follows, see Figure 6.11:

- propose the retrieved cases to the user in order to make a choice;

- ask for the user for:

  - specific requirements on the selected case;

  - a certain price threshold or an allowed degradation of the price (specified as certain limits);

  - a delivery time threshold or an allowed degradation of the delivery time (specified as certain limits);

Example – Applying Degradation and Threshold for Adapting Cases

We now give examples of how degradation and threshold apply to solution adaptation when the domain knowledge is represented as a Soft CSP.

---

[2] Usually the fuzzy CSP is represented by the semiring $< [0, 1], max, min, 0, 1 >$, but for modeling this example we had chosen a similar one which uses the opposite order.

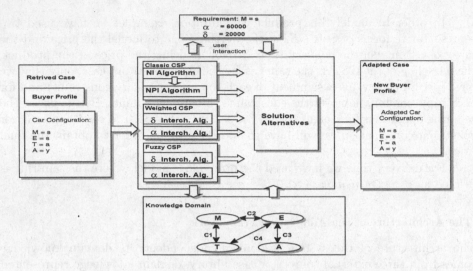

Figure 6.11: Adaptation engine based on Soft $CSPs$.

The product catalog can represent the available choices through a Soft $CSPs$, as shown in Figure 6.10. By different representations of the semiring, the CSP represents different problem formulations. Thus, in order to model the cost of the product a weighted CSP representation might be the most appropriate. In a weighted CSP, the semiring values model the cost of different components and their integration. Formally, the semiring operations and values in a weighted CSP are: $< \Re^+, min, +, +\infty, 0 >$. This allows one to model optimization problems where the goal is to minimize the total cost of the proposed solution. The cost of the solution is computed by summing up the costs of all the constraints. The goal is to find the n–tuples (where n is the number of all the variables) which minimize the total sum of the costs of their subtuples (one for each constraint).

In Figure 6.12, we present a solution adaptation example of the product configuration relative to its delivery costs. The product is modeled in terms of a weighted CSP as in Figure 6.10. The cost of the current solution is 18 and the user request is to update the value of the engine, here represented by variable E. By allowing a degradation of the solution with $\delta = 0$ the solution updates the variable E to value s and its cost decreases to 17. By allowing a degradation of $\delta = 4$ the current solution can adapt its variable E either to value s or d where the cost decreases to 17 or increases to 22 respectively. Thus, among the values of variable E, we find that for degradation $\delta = 0$, value s is ^{0}substitutable to values l and d, and value l is ^{0}substitutable to d. For a degradation $\delta = 1$, values s and l are ^{1}interchangeable and ^{1}substitutable to d, respectively. By allowing a degradation $\delta = 4$, values s and l are ^{4}interchangeable, values l and d are ^{4}interchangeable and value s is ^{4}substitutable to value d. For a degradation $\delta > 5$ all the values of E variable are $^\delta$interchangeable.

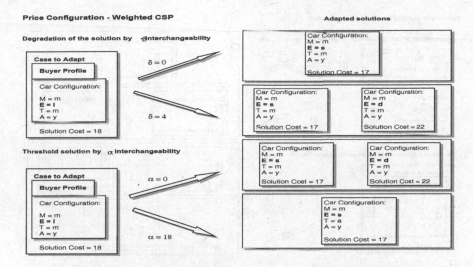

Figure 6.12: Example of solution adaptation based on δ and α interchangeability where the knowledge domain is represented as a weighted $CSPs$.

When searching for solutions to a soft CSP, it is possible to gain efficiency by not distinguishing values that could in any case not be part of a solution of sufficient quality. In $_\alpha$interchangeability, two values are interchangeable if they do not affect the quality of any solution with quality better than α, called the *threshold* factor. In our price modeling example, see Figure 6.12 we can see that for a threshold $\alpha = 0$, the solution can be updated for the variable E with all the other values of its domains as all its values are $_0$interchangeable; this is explained by the fact that since there are no solutions better than $\alpha = 0$, by definition all the elements are interchangeable. For a certain threshold $\alpha = 18$, values l and d are $_{18}$interchangeable and value s can substitute value l or value d. And for higher α, value s can substitute value l or value d and value l can substitute value d.

For modeling the delivery time of the car we had used as optimization criterion a fuzzy CSP. Fuzzy CSP associate a preference level with each tuple of values. This level is usually between 0 and 1 and expresses how much the tuple of values satisfy the constraint, where 1 represents the best value (that is the tuple is the most preferred and complete satisfaction) and 0 the worst (no satisfaction). The semiring $< [0,1], max, min, 0, 1 >$ models the fuzzy CSP type, see Chapter 3. In our example, we had modeled the delivery time with the semiring $< \Re^+, min, max, +\infty, 0 >$ which is similar to the fuzzy one, but uses an inverse order. Let us call it *opposite fuzzy*. Delay in delivery time is determined by the time taken to obtain components and to reserve the resources for the assembly process. For the delivery time of the car, only the longest delay would matter. In Figure 6.13, the solution we have to adapt has a delivery time of 7 days but the user would prefer to change the engine type of the car. For a degradation of the

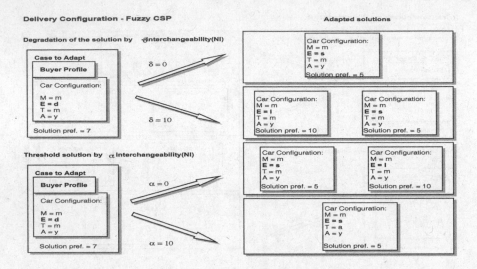

Figure 6.13: Example of solution adaptation based on δ and α interchangeability where the knowledge domain is represented as a Fuzzy CSP.

solution $\delta = 0$, we can adapt the solution only by value s for variable E, where the delivery time goes to 5 days. By allowing a higher degradation of the solution to $\delta = 10$, there are two possible solution adaptations: when variable E takes value s the delivery time stays the same, while when it takes value l the delivery time increases to 10 days. For $\delta = 0$, value s is [0]substitutable for values l and d of variable E, while for $\delta = 7$, values s and d are becoming [7]interchangeable. For $\delta = 10$, all values of variable E are [10]interchangeable.

Computing adaptation by $_\alpha$interchangeability for this fuzzy example allows the adaptation of the solution, see Figure 6.13, to value s and as well as to value l of variable E. This happens because all the values are interchangeable for a threshold $\alpha = 0$. For a threshold $\alpha = 7$, values l and d stay interchangeable, but value s can only substitute value l and value d, while for higher values of α threshold, value s can substitute values l and d and only value d can substitute value l.

6.7   Related Work

We proposed a generic framework to realize case adaptation for the domain of problems which can be represented as crisp or Soft $CSPs$.

There are some other approaches to viewing the adaptation problem as a constraint satisfaction problem. One of them was published by Purvis and Pu in [76] for a case–based design problem where the adaptation process is based on the constraints over discrete $CSPs$. Their methodology formalizes the case adaptation process in the sense of combining multiple cases to achieve the solution of the new problem, by applying repair–based CSP algorithm proposed by Minton in [80]. This method relies only on the knowledge accumulated in the case base whereas the interchangeability–based method proposed by us also considers information offered by the domain knowledge formulated as a CSP. The approaches are different because, in the method proposed by Purvis and Pu [76] the constraints between specific values of the variables are stored in the case, while the adaptation method based on interchangeability proposed by us stores in the case only the solution of the new problem, while the constraints between variables are held in an external module which contains the domain knowledge. We believe that our approach gives more flexibility to the adaptation module, but in the future it would be interesting to study how the two methods can be combined for improving the adaptation process.

By extending the framework to the Soft CSP domain and thus, allowing preferences, the flexibility of the framework is further improved.

Another approach to adaptation with constraints where the solution of a new problem is built by satisfying the new constraints and by transforming a memorized solution was published by Hua, Faltings and Smith in [54]. They proposed a case–based reasoner for architectural design where constraints restrict numerical relationships among dimensions. This is called $CADRE$. CADRE introduced the concept of *dimensional reduction*: before attempting to adapt a case, it constructs an explicit representation of the degrees of freedom available for adaptation. The adaptation method based on *dimensional reduction* has been tested successfully in the IDIOM project [53]. However, CADRE defined this approach only for numeric constraints. In our approach we study the domain of discrete CSP which cannot be solved by a numeric approach.

In the domain of discrete variables, the adaptation space is less obvious. We proposed here a method based on interchangeability for domains of problems which can be expressed as crisp and soft $CSPs$ which localize changes in discrete spaces and thus offers a reliable method for determining the closest solution.

Chapter 7

Conclusions

This chapter outlines the main results and contributions of this study.

Important features of intelligent agent systems are the reasoning methods applied during their decision process. There are many decisions which an agent has to take: either externally, in reaction to the environment such as what event to react to, or internally, for decisions such as which goal to pursue, how to pursue the desired goal and when to suspend/abandon the goal, or change to another goal.

The decision making process can be naturally expressed in terms of constraint satisfaction problems.

Moreover, agents need to construct or adapt plans for achieving their goals. When an event from the environment occurs the agent looks for relevant plans, which can respond to this type of event. For each relevant plan, the agent examines how appropriate the plan is for the current situation and then the agent selects, adapts and starts executing the most appropriate plan found.

Planning is one of the reasoning methods which can be solved through constraint satisfaction methods. Our specific interest focused during this research on adaptation techniques. The adaptation process can be a complex one and sometimes might require the same search effort as solving the problem from the scratch. In this work we have studied how and when it is appropriate depending on the problem structure to adapt already known plans/solutions based on a constraint satisfaction technique called *interchangeability*. Interchangeability is a general concept for formalizing and breaking symmetries in $CSPs$. We focus on partial and soft interchangeability in discrete $CSPs$, algorithms for interchangeability computation and its application to problems such as case adaptation.

7.1   Contributions

Constraint satisfaction problems techniques have proven to be a generic framework for modeling a wide range of problems such as configuration, diagnosis, scheduling, decision making and planning.

Constraint satisfaction framework is appropriate for modelling and solving agent reasoning problems such as decision making and planning. We focus our research on adaptation process in constraint– and case–based reasoning systems and its application in software agent.

For realizing adaptation, we have studied constraint satisfaction methods based on interchangeability for solutions adaptation and update.

The main topics and aspects driven in this research are:

- How partial interchangeability can be approximated based on local neighborhoods;

- Definitions and algorithms for interchangeability in soft $CSPs$;

- Interchangeability computation in distributed environments based on collaborative agents;

- Solution adaptation in dynamic environments;

- A generic framework for case adaptation based on constraint satisfaction techniques.

In the following we discuss the contribution for each of these aspects and the obtained results.

7.1.1   Partial Interchangeability

The major contribution in Chapter 2 consists of novel algorithms for computing minimal, and globally minimum dependent sets which localize change in CSP solutions.

We gave a sound algorithm for computing a minimal set of variables which might have to change to allow interchange in the critical variable. The algorithm for computing this minimal dependent set (MDS) is a constructive algorithm based on discrimination tree structures; it searches incrementally for the dependent set, which enlarges with the spreading of the change in the CSP. We have proven that for a given interchange there can be many minimal dependent sets. The MDS algorithm finds one of them based on heuristics which minimize the number of variables to be included in the further dependent set. As the MDS algorithm finds the minimal dependent set using heuristic search, it is not able to find the global minimum.

There are multiple ways a change can propagate and while there are many minimal dependent sets only few are minimum ones. We gave a complete and sound algorithm for finding the minimum dependent sets among the minimal ones. The completeness of this algorithm trades off on efficiency but we show that it can be used efficiently in sparse $CSPs$ up to a certain neighboring distance from the critical variable.

Otherwise, the minimal dependent set algorithm can be used and by applying this algorithm to randomly generated problems, we have gained an understanding of the existence and size of minimal dependent sets according to the problem structure:

- Strong dependency on the density parameter of the CSP, where MDS are more frequent in $CSPs$ with high density. This complements the neighborhood interchangeability which occurs more often in sparse $CSPs$.

- Weak dependency on the domain sizes where the domain partitions of variables in the MDS set increases with the number of resources.

On the basis of this work we believe that partial interchangeability characterized by minimal and minimum dependent sets has potential in practical applications, i.e. for identifying classes of equivalent solutions as a basis for adaptation. Moreover, agent reasoning can use these adaptation techniques to adjust agent plans and improve the decision making process.

7.1.2 Tuple Interchangeability

We defined a new concept of partial interchangeability which we call *Neighborhood Tuple Interchangeability (NTI)* which characterizes partial interchangeability better then the minimal/minimum dependent sets, as it guarantees that the assignments are valid among the variables of the dependent set. We gave a sound and complete algorithm for finding equivalent partial solutions, which we call *neighborhood interchangeable tuples*. This algorithm is based on the concept of *Neighborhood Tuple Interchangeability*, which turns out to be more useful for adapting solutions than Neighborhood Partial Interchangeability as it can find already consistent interchangeable tuples for variables in the dependent set, if they exist.

The NTI method can improve the solution adaptation process in agent reasoning with more precision. Where dependent sets are just identifying the set of variables and their domain partitions to which the change localize, without guarantee of solutions inside this set, NTI can find already consistent tuples of the dependent set to be interchanged.

We showed that NTI can approximate correctly PI and gave the algorithm for its computation. We proved that if a set is found not to be NTI, then it can also be guaranteed to not be partially interchangeable at all. So, we have a complete method to compute partial interchangeable values, however it does not necessarily find the smallest NTI dependent sets. The algorithm can be extended in a straightforward manner to be complete by realizing exhaustive search among all the alternatives, but it might trade off too much effectiveness for its completeness.

In experimental evaluation on randomly generated problems, we found that in general most values seem to become interchangeable with dependent sets of manageable size, where they increase with the CSP density. While the complexity of our methods is exponential in the size of the dependent sets, we do not expect this to be a great problem in practice.

7.1.3   Definitions and Algorithms for Soft Interchangeability

We have defined interchangeability for the Soft CSP framework and we have given polynomial algorithms for its computation. In soft CSP, we can relax the symmetries based on the semiring values. We have defined two new forms of more relaxed interchangeability based on soft CSP properties. α–interchangeability uses threshold α in order to eliminate distinctions that would not interest us anyway, while δ–interchangeability specifies how precisely we want to optimize our solution.

We have shown that all the properties of classical $CSPs$ can be extended to the soft case. We have studied the occurrence of $(^{\delta}/_{\alpha})$Neighborhood Interchangeability (NI) and $(^{\delta}/_{\alpha})$Neighborhood Partial Interchangeability (NPI) depending on the problem structure and we have evaluated how their occurrence depends on the values of threshold α and degradation δ. In our tests, we evaluated also how much local NI corresponds to *Full Interchangeability (FI)*. The experimental facts showed that there is high occurrence of $(_{\alpha})$NI and $(^{\delta})$NI interchangeability around optimal solutions of Soft $CSPs$. Thus, these algorithms can be used successfully in solution update applications as we showed for example in case adaptation. Moreover, we also showed that NI interchangeability can well approximate FI interchangeability.

We believe that the results prove the reliability for using $(^{\delta}/_{\alpha})$interchangeability for practical applications.

7.1.4   Interchangeability Solving Collaborative Agents in Distributed Systems

When the CSP problem knowledge is distributed among different locations, the centralized algorithms for its solving can no longer be applied. New algorithmic techniques had to be proposed for solving $CSPs$ when they are distributed.

For the domain of distributed $CSPs$ we propose algorithms for computing neighborhood and partial interchangeability. These algorithms are based on collaborative agents which share the work required to solve the CSP, and its interchangeability computation respectively.

We proposed distributed algorithms for the computation of neighborhood interchangeability and partial interchangeability characterized by the dependent sets. Distributed $CSPs$ computing involves a number of new issues to be considered such as: how the tasks can be usefully divided among agents, how one agent can exploit the knowledge generated by the others, and how the agents communicate with each other. Addressing all these issues we have shown that the computation of interchangeability, neighborhood or partial, is possible in distributed environments.

7.1.5 Interchangeability Solving in Dynamic Environments

Significant research work has involved static CSP where all the knowledge about the problem including variables, their domain of values and the constraints between them, are known before the computation starts and do not change with time. This is not the case for many real world applications in which all the CSP knowledge may change in time. Also, for software agents environments, the need to have all the problem domain knowledge before the computation begins is too strict.

These aspects motivated our research for interchangeability algorithms in dynamic $CSPs$. Adapting previously known solutions is a major issue for $CSPs$ in dynamic environments, since one might not need to compute the problem from scratch when a solution is already known and can be adapted to the changes in the CSP, i.e. a constraint restriction or relaxation.

We have shown how neighborhood and partial interchangeability can be computed in dynamic $CSPs$ environments. Moreover, we present algorithms for adapting solutions in dynamic $CSPs$. Based on the results obtained in Chapter 2, we know when it is appropriate to adapt solutions rather than computing it from scratch based on the CSP problem structure.

7.1.6 Generic Case Adaptation

When an agent needs to recall the approach it has used in solving previous problems, another reasoning technique such as case based reasoning can be applied. When a new problem has to be solved, the closest known one is retrieved and adapted to the new requirements. The adaptation process proves to be difficult and domain dependent. In this part of the work we addressed problems regarding the adaptation process in case based reasoning systems where the knowledge domain can be represented as constraint satisfaction. Based on constraint satisfaction and interchangeability properties we proposed a generic method for case adaptation.

We presented how NI and NTI interchangeability forms can be used for adapting solutions during the case adaptation process.

Moreover, we extended our generic tool for the knowledge domains which can be represented as Soft $CSPs$. Based on interchangeability concepts defined in Soft $CSPs$, we provided methods for solution adaptation.

We presented how the adaptation based on interchangeability applies to a CBR system for product configuration. However, the framework works in the same way for all the problems which can be represented as CSP. The CBR system we presented functions as a sales manager system, which contains cases representing past sales and consisting of buyer profiles and the chosen product. Admissible configurations can be precisely specified as $CSPs$, but each customer has particular needs that remain largely unformalized. We use CBR to map properties of the customer to these implicit customer needs and product configurations that fit them. The configuration of the product is modeled as a CSP. Interchangeability and constraint satisfaction techniques are used to adapt the proposed solution by the CBR system to customer requirements and preferences. We use standard $CSPs$ to model strict constraints of product configuration where costs and preferences are modeled with soft $CSPs$. For adapting a case we apply all form of interchangeability.

By grouping together constraint satisfaction methods for adapting solutions over continuous domains based on *dimensionality reduction* and over discrete domains based on *interchangeability*, where we provide methods for hard and soft constraints as well, we can provide a generic tool for case adaptation.

7.2   Further research

In future work, the algorithms for computing partial interchangeability can be further improved or extended in order to be applied in more complex agent environments. Some of the goals are:

- To study efficiency and applicability of minimal/minimum dependent set algorithms for larger inputs, i.e. sets of variables and their corresponding sets of values to be interchanged. When an agent needs to adapt a solution not only for one critical variable but many, new efficient algorithms need to be found.

- To study how the occurrence of interchangeability is affected by the evolution of a dynamic CSP and how the search in dynamic CSP can be improved by interchangeability. More effort should be given to studying how interchangeability aspects for solution location are affected in an agent environment which evolves dynamically.

- To study how interchangeability improves search in Soft $CSPs$, algorithms for computing NTI in Soft $CSPs$ and their application in distributed environments.

Many possible applications of interchangeability are mentioned in Chapter 1. In future research, we believe that partial interchangeability can be further exploited in:

- Problem abstraction and reformulation, where interchangeable tuples or a critical variable and its dependent set for making its domain interchangeable provide meaningful meta–variables.

- Distributed problem solving, where it is possible to limit the set of agents that a change has to be coordinated with, and also to make local changes so that they do not spread through the entire problem.

- Structuring and classifying solution based on the dependent sets where the changes are localized.

- Interactive systems, where it is possible to show what parts of a solution might be affected by a local change.

7.3 Final Conclusion

Techniques for agent reasoning based on constraint satisfaction methods have been studied in this work. Constraint satisfaction is an appropriate technique for modeling decision making and planning processes in agents. Moreover, agents need to adapt their plans for achieving goals. This research work concerns solution adaptation methods based on interchangeability in constraint satisfaction problems.

Most work in constraint satisfaction has focused on efficiently generating solutions. However, it is also interesting how solutions can be adapted and abstracted. Interchangeability is an interesting concept for this. In this research, we have addressed two open problems: we have given a practical algorithm for approximating partial interchangeability, and we have given definitions and algorithms for interchangeability in soft CSP. Both are useful for case adaptation and abstraction of solution spaces in general.

Bibliography

[1] A. Aamodt and E. Plaza. CBR Tutorial. http://www.iiia.csic.es/People/enric/AICom.html, 1994.

[2] F. Bacchus and P. van Beek. On the conversion between non-binary and binary constraint satisfaction problems. In *Proceedings of the 15th Conference of the American Association of Artificial Intelligence (AAAI-98)*, pages 311–318, 1998.

[3] B. Bastani. A survey of dynamic csp. *Technical report, Intelligent System Laboratory, Simon Fraser University*, 2003.

[4] F. Bellifemine, A. Poggi, and G. Rimassa. Developing multi agent systems with a fipa-compliant agent framework. In *Software Practice and Experience*, 2001.

[5] B.W. Benson and E. Freuder. Interchangeability preprocessing can improve forward checking search. In *Proc. of the 10th ECAI, Vienna, Austria*, pages 28–30, 1992.

[6] C. Bessière. Arc-consistency in dynamic constraint satisfaction problems. In *Proceeding of the Ninth National Conference on Artificial Intelligence*, pages 221–226, 1991.

[7] C. Bessiere. Arc-consistency and arc-consistency again. *Artificial Intelligence*, 65, 1994.

[8] S. Bistarelli. *Soft Constraint Solving and programming: a general framework*. PhD thesis, Dipartimento di Informatica, Università di Pisa, Italy, mar 2001. TD-2/01.

[9] S. Bistarelli, B. Faltings, and N. Neagu. A definition of interchangeability for soft csps. In *Proc. of the Joint Workshop of the ERCIM Working Group on Constraints and the CologNet area on Constraint and Logic Programming on Constraint Solving and Constraint Logic Programming - Selected Papers*, LNAI. Springer-Verlag, 2002.

[10] S. Bistarelli, B. Faltings, and N. Neagu. Interchangeability in soft csps. In *Proc. of the 8th CP-2002*, LNCS. Springer-Verlag, 2002.

[11] S. Bistarelli, H. Fargier, U. Montanari, F. Rossi, T. Schiex, and G. Verfaillie. Semiring-based CSPs and valued CSPs: Basic properties and comparison. In *Over-Constrained Systems*, number 1106 in LNCS. Springer-Verlag, 1996.

[12] S. Bistarelli, H. Fargier, U. Montanari, F. Rossi, T. Schiex, and G. Verfaillie. Semiring-based CSPs and Valued CSPs: Frameworks, properties, and comparison. *CONSTRAINTS: An international journal. Kluwer*, 4(3), 1999.

[13] S. Bistarelli, U. Montanari, and F. Rossi. Constraint Solving over Semirings. In *Proc. IJCAI95*, San Francisco, CA, USA, 1995. Morgan Kaufman.

[14] S. Bistarelli, U. Montanari, and F. Rossi. Semiring-based Constraint Solving and Optimization. *Journal of the ACM*, 44(2):201–236, Mar 1997.

[15] S. Bistarelli, U. Montanari, and F. Rossi. Semiring-based Constraint Solving and Optimization. *Journal of ACM.*, 44, n.2:201–236, 1997.

[16] S. Bistarelli, U. Montanari, and F. Rossi. Semiring-based Constraint Logic Programming: Syntax and Semantics. *ACM Transactions on Programming Languages and System (TOPLAS)*, 23:1–29, jan 2001.

[17] S. Bistarelli, U. Montanari, and F. Rossi. Soft concurrent constraint programming. In *Proc. ESOP, April 6 - 14, 2002, Grenoble, France*, LNCS. Springer-Verlag, 2002.

[18] C. Brown, L. Finkelstein, and P. Purdom. Backtracking Searching in the Preasence of Symmetry. In *Applied Algebra, Algebraic Algorithms and Erroe-Correcting Codes*, pages 99–110. Springer Verlag, 1988.

[19] D. Lesaint C. D. Elfe, E. C. Freuder. Dynamic constraint satisfaction for feature interaction. *BT Technology Journal*, 16, 1998.

[20] R. Schank C. Riesbeck. Inside case-based reasoning. In *Lawrence Erlbaum*, 1989.

[21] M. Calisti. *Coordination and Negotiation for Solving Multi-Provider Service Provisioning*. PhD thesis, Artificial Intelligence Laboratory - Swiss Federal Institute of technology of Lausanne, 2001.

[22] Stuart W. Chalmers. *Agents and Constraint Logic*. PhD thesis, Department of Computing Science, University of Aberdeen, UK, 2004.

[23] H. Chalupsky, Y. Gil, C. A. Knoblock, K. Lerman, D.V. Pynadath J. Oh, T.A. Russ, and M. Tambe. Electric elves: Applying agent technology to support human organizations. In *Proceedings of Innovative Applications of Artificial Intelligence Conference*, 2001.

[24] B. Choueiry and B. Faltings. Using Abstractions Resource Allocation. In *In IEEE 1995 International Conference on Robotics and Automation*, pages 1027–1033, Nagoya, Japan, 1995.

[25] B. Choueiry, B. Faltings, and R. Weigel. Abstraction by Interchangeability in Resource Allocation. In *Proc. of the 14 th IJCAI-95*, pages 1694–1701, Montreal, Canada, 1995.

[26] B. Y. Choueiry. *Abstraction Methods for Resource Allocation.* PhD thesis, Thesis no. 1292, Artificial Intelligence Laboratory - Swiss Federal Institute of technology of Lausanne (EPFL), 1994.

[27] B. Y. Choueiry and A. M. Davis. Dynamic Bundling: Less Effort for More Solutions. In Sven Koenig and Robert Holte, editors, *5th International Symposium on Abstraction, Reformulation and Approximation (SARA 2002)*, volume 2371 of *Lecture Notes in Artificial Intelligence*, pages 64–82. Springer Verlag, 2002.

[28] B. Y. Choueiry and G. Noubir. On the computation of local interchangeability in discrete constraint satisfaction problems. In *Proc. of AAAI-98*, pages 326–333, Madison, Wiscowsin, 1998.

[29] Berthe Y. Choueiry and Amy M. Beckwith. On Finding the First Solution Bundle in Finite Constraint Satisfaction Problems. In University of Nebraska, editor, *Technical Report CSL-01-03. consystlab.unl.edu/CSL-01-04.ps*, 2001.

[30] Z. Collin, R. Dechter, and S. Katz. On the Feasibility of Distributed Constraint Satisfaction. In *Proceedings of the Twelfth International Joint Conference on Artificial Intelligence, IJCAI-91, Sidney, Australia*, pages 318–324, 1991.

[31] M. Cooper. Reduction operations in fuzzy or valued constraint satisfaction. *Fuzzy Sets and Systems*, 134(3), 2003.

[32] R. Debruyne. Arc-consistency in dynamic csps is no more prohibitive. *Proceedings of the 8th International Conference on Tools with Artificial Intelligence (ICTAI '96)*, 1996.

[33] R. Dechter and A. Dechter. Belief maintenance in dynamic constraint networks. In *Proceedings of the Seventh Annual Conference of the American Association of Artificial Intelligence*, pages 37–42, 1988.

[34] D. Dubois, H. Fargier, and H. Prade. The calculus of fuzzy restrictions as a basis for flexible constraint satisfaction. In *Proc. IEEE International Conference on Fuzzy Systems*, pages 1131–1136. IEEE, 1993.

[35] Barry Richards E. Thomas Richards. Nogood learning for constraint satisfaction. *Proceedings CP 96 Workshop on Constraint Programming Applications*, 1996.

[36] T. Ellman. Abstraction via Approximate Symmetry. In *In Proc. of the 13th IJCAI*, pages 916–921, Chambery, France, 1993.

[37] P. Faratin. *Automated Service Negotiation Between Autonomous Compu-tational Agents*. PhD thesis, University of London, Queen Mary College, Department of Electronic Engineering, 2000.

[38] H. Fargier and J. Lang. Uncertainty in constraint satisfaction problems: a probabilistic approach. In *Proc. European Conference on Symbolic and Qualitative Approaches to Reasoning and Uncertainty (ECSQARU)*, volume 747 of *LNCS*, pages 97–104. Springer-Verlag, 1993.

[39] J. Fillmore and S. Williamson. On Backtracking: A Combinatorial Descrip-tion of the Algorithm. In *SIAM Journal of Computing 3(1)*, pages 41–55, 1974.

[40] E. Freuder. *Constraint-based Reasoning*. MIT Press, 1994.

[41] E. C. Freuder. Eliminating Interchangeable Values in Constraint Satisfaction Problems. In *In Proc. of AAAI-91*, pages 227–233, Anaheim, CA, 1991.

[42] E. C. Freuder. Eliminating interchangeable values in constraint satisfaction problems. In *Proc. of AAAI-91*, pages 227–233, Anaheim, CA, 1991.

[43] E. C. Freuder and D. Sabin. Interchangeability Supports Abstraction and Reformulation for Multi-Dimensional Constraint Satisfaction. In *In Proc. of AAAI-96*, pages 191–196, Portland, 1996.

[44] E.C. Freuder and R.J. Wallace. Partial constraint satisfaction. *AI Journal*, 58, 1992.

[45] E. Gelle, B. V. Faltings, and I.F.C. Smith. Structural engineering design support by constraint satisfaction. In *Artificial Intelligence in Design 2000*, pages 311–331. Kluwer Academic Publishers, 2000.

[46] K. Ghedira and G. Verfaillie. A multi-agent model for the resource alloca-tion problem: A reactive approach. In *Procceedings of the Tenth European COnference on Artificial Intelligence*, pages 252–254, 1992.

[47] J. Glaisher. On the Problem of the Eight Queens. In *Philosophical Magazine, series 4, 48*, pages 457–467, 1974.

[48] A. Haselbock. Exploiting interchangeabilities in constraint satisfaction prob-lems. In *Proc. of the 13th IJCAI*, pages 282–287, 1993.

[49] P. Van Hentenryck. Generality versus Specificity: An Experience with AI and OR Techniques. *In AAAI-88: Proceedings National Conference on Artificial Intelligence*, pages 660–664, 1988.

[50] P. Van Hentenryck, P. Flener, J. Pearson, and M. Agren. Tractable symme-try breaking for csps with interchangeable values. In *Proc. of 18 th IJCAI*, pages 277–285, 2003.

[51] K. Hirayama and M. Yokoo. An approach to over-constrained distributed constraint satisfaction problems: Distributed hierarchical constraint satisfaction. In *4th International Conference on Multi-agent Systems (ICMAS-2000)*, 2000.

[52] K. Hirayama and Makoto Yokoo. Distributed partial constraint satisfaction problem. In *Principles and Practice of Constraint Programming*, pages 222–236, 1997.

[53] C. Lottaz I. Smith and B.Faltings. Spatial composition using cases: IDIOM. *In Proc. of the 1st International Conference in CBR, pages 88-97*, 1995.

[54] B. Faltings K. Hua and I. Smith. CADRE: case-based geometric design. *In Artificial Intelligence in Engineering 10, pages 171-183*, 1996.

[55] J. Kolodner. An introduction to case-based reasoning. In *Artificial Intelligence Review 6(1)*, 1992.

[56] H. Krautz and B. Selman. Planning as Satisfiability. *In Proc. of the 10 th Ecai, pages 359-363, Vienna, Austria*, 1992.

[57] A. Lal and B. Y. Choueiry. Dynamic Detection and Exploitation of Value Symmetries for Non-Binary Finite CSPs. In *Third International Workshop on Symmetry in Constraint Satisfaction Problems (SymCon'03)*, pages 112–126, Kinsale, County Cork, Ireland, 2003.

[58] D. Leake. Case-Based Reasoning: Experiences, Lessons and Future Directions. In *AAAI Press*, 1996.

[59] David Leake. Case Based Reasoning in context: The present and future. Technical report, 1996.

[60] V.R. Lesser. An overview of dai: Viewing distributed ai as distributed search. In *Journal of Japanese Society for Artificial Intelligence*, 1990.

[61] M. Wooldridge. *An Introduction to Multiagent Systems*. John Wiley and Sons Ltd., 2002.

[62] A. K. Mackworth. Consistency in Networks of Relations. *Artificial Intelligence 8, pages 99-118*, 1977.

[63] A. K. Mackworth. Constraint-based Design of Embeded Intelligent Systems. *In Constraints 2(1), pages 83-86, Vienna, Austria*, 1992.

[64] A. K. Mackworth. Constraint-based agents: The abc's of cba's. In *Proc. of Principles and Practice of Constraint Programming (CP)*, LNCS. Springer-Verlag, 2000.

[65] Alan Mackworth. Constraint satisfaction. In Stuart C. Shapiro, editor, *Encyclopedia of Artificial Intelligence*, pages 285–293. Wiley, 1992. Volume 1, second edition.

[66] I. Miguel and Q. Shen. Dynamic flexible constraint satisfaction. *Applied Intelligence*, 13, 2000.

[67] P. J. Modi, W.-M. Shen, M. Tambe, and M. Yokoo. ADOPT: Asynchronous Distributed Constraint Optimization with Quality Guarantees. *Artificial Intelligence Journal*, 2004.

[68] N. Neagu and B. Faltings. Constraint Satisfaction for Case Adaptation. *In Proc. of the Workshop on Case Adaptation in ICCBR-99, Munich.*, 1999.

[69] N. Neagu and B. Faltings. Exploiting interchangeabilities for case adaptation. In *In Proc. of the 4th ICCBR01*, 2001.

[70] B. Nebel and J. Koehler. Plan reuse versus plan generation: A theoretical and empirical analysis. In *Artificial Intelligence*, pages 427–454, 1995.

[71] Y. Nishibe, K. Kuwabara, T. Ishida, and M. Yokoo. Speed-up of distributed constraint satisfaction and its application to communication network path assignments, 1994.

[72] V. Parunak, A. Ward, M. Fleicher, J. Sauter, and T. Chang. Distributed component-centered design as agent based distributed constraint optimization. In *IEEE Trans. on Knowledge and Data Engineering*, pages 673–685, Madison, Wiscowsin, 1998.

[73] Adrian Petcu and Boi Faltings. Applying interchangeability techniques to the distributed breakout algorithm. In AAAI, editor, *Proceedings of the International Joint Conference on Artificial Intelligence 2003*, IJCAII P. O. Box 5490 Somerset, NJ 08875, USA, 2003. IJCAI, Inc., Morgan Kaufmann Publishers, San Francisco, USA.

[74] J.-F. Puget. On the Satisfiability of Symmetrical Constrained Satisfaction Problems. In *In Proc. of ISMIS*, pages 350–361, 1993.

[75] L. Purvis. *Intelligent Design Problem Solving Using Case-Based and Constraint-Based Techniques*. PhD thesis, University of Connecticut, 1995.

[76] L. Purvis and P. Pu. Adaptation using Constraint Satisfaction Techniques. *In Proc. of the 1st International Conference in CBR, pages 88-97*, 1995.

[77] N. Roos, Y. Ran, and H. Jaap van den Herik. Combining local search and constraint propagation to find a minimal change solution for a dynamic csp. *Proceedings of the 9th International Conference on Artificial Intelligence: Methodology, Systems, and Applications*, 2000.

[78] F. Rossi and I. Pilar. Abstracting Soft Constraints: Some Experimental Results. In *Joint Annual ERCIM/CoLogNet Workshop on Constraint and Logic Programming*, Budapest, Hungary, 2003.

[79] Zs. Ruttkay. Fuzzy constraint satisfaction. In *Proc. 3rd IEEE International Conference on Fuzzy Systems*, pages 1263–1268, 1994.

[80] A. Philips S. Minton, M. Johnson and P. Laird. Minimizing Conflicts: A Heuristic Repair Method for Constraint Satisfaction and Scheduling Problems. *In Artificial Intelligence 58, pages 88-97*, 1995.

[81] T. Schiex. Possibilistic constraint satisfaction problems, or "how to handle soft constraints?". In *Proc. 8th Conf. of Uncertainty in AI*, pages 269–275, 1992.

[82] T. Schiex. Possibilistic constraint satisfaction problems, or "how to handle soft constraints?". In *Proc. 8th Conf. of Uncertainty in AI*, 1992.

[83] T. Schiex, H. Fargier, and G. Verfaille. Valued Constraint Satisfaction Problems: Hard and Easy Problems. In *Proc. IJCAI95*, pages 631–637, San Francisco, CA, USA, 1995. Morgan Kaufmann.

[84] T. Schiex and G. Verfaillie. Nogood recording for static and dynamic constraint satisfaction problems. *International Journal of Artificial Intelligence Tools*, 3, 1994.

[85] W.-M. Shen and M. Yim. Self-reconfigurable robots. In *IEEE Transactions on Mechatronics*, 2002.

[86] M.-C. Silaghi, D. Sam-Haroud, and B. Faltings. Asynchronous search with aggregations. In *In Proceedings of AAAI.*, pages 917–922, 2000.

[87] Marius-Calin Silaghi, D. Sam-Haroud, and B. Faltings. Distributed asynchronous search with private constraints. In *Proc. of AA2000*, pages 177–178, Barcelona, June 2000.

[88] S Slade. Case-based reasoning: A research paradigm. In *AI Magazine Spring*, 1991.

[89] M. Tambe. Towards flexible teamwork. In *Journal of Artificial Intelligence Research*, pages 83–124, 1997.

[90] P. van Hentenryck. Incremental search in constraint logic programming. *New Generation Computing*, 9, 1991.

[91] G. Verfaillie and T. Schiex. Solution reuse in dynamic constraint satisfaction problems. In *Proceedings of the Twelfth Conference of the American Association of Artificial Intelligence*, pages 307–312, 1994.

[92] M. Wallace. Applying constraints for scheduling. *In Constraint Programming, volume 131 of NATO ASI Series Advanced Science Institute Series.* Springer Verlag, 1994.

[93] Mark Wallace. Practical applications of constraint programming. *Constraints*, 1(1/2):139–168, 1996.

[94] D. Waltz. Understanding line drawings of scenes with shadows. In Patrick H. Winston, editor, *The Psychology of Computer Vision*. McGraw-Hill, 1975.

[95] R. Weigel. *Dynamic Abstractions and Reformulations in Constraint Satis-
      faction Problems.* PhD thesis, Thesis no. 1825, Artificial Intelligence Labo-
      ratory - Swiss Federal Institute of technology of Lausanne (EPFL), 1998.

[96] R. Weigel and B. Faltings. Structuring Techniques for Constraint Satisfac-
      tion Problems. *In Proceedings of the 15 th IJCAI,* 1997.

[97] R. Weigel and B. Faltings. Interchangeability for Case Adaptation in Con-
      figuration Problems. *In Proceedings of the AAAI98 Spring Symposium on
      Multimodal Reasoning, Stanford, CA, TR SS-98-04.,* 1998.

[98] R. Weigel and B. Faltings. Compiling Constraint Satisfaction Problems.
      Artificial Intelligence 115, pg. 257-287., 1999.

[99] R. Weigel, B. Faltings, and B.Y. Choueiry. Context in discrete satisfaction
      problems. In *12th ECAIA,* pages 205–209, Budapest, Hungary, 1996.

[100] G. Weiss. *Multiagent Systems: A Modern Approach to Distributed Artificial
      Intelligence.* MIT Press, 1999.

[101] S. Willmott, M. Calisti, and B. Faltings. CCL: Expressions of Choice in
      Agent Communication and Macho-Gonzalez S. and Belakhdar O. and Tor-
      rens M. In *Proceedings of the Fourth International Conference on Multi
      Agent Systems (ICMAS-2000).* IEEE Press (in print), 2000.

[102] M. Wooldridge and N.R. Jennings. Intelligent agents: Theory and practice.
      The Knowledge Engineering Review, 10(2):115–152, 1995.

[103] R. Dechter Y. El Fattah. Diagnosing tree-decomposable circuits. *In Proc.
      of the 14 th IJCAI, pg. 1742-1748,* 1995.

[104] M. Yokoo. Asynchronous weak-commitment search for solving distributed
      constraint satisfaction problems. In *First International Conference on Prin-
      ciples and Practice of Constraint Programming (CP-95),* 1995.

[105] M. Yokoo and E. Durfee. Distributed constraint satisfaction for formalizing
      distributed problem solving. In *12th International Conference on Distributed
      Computing Systems (ICDCS-92),* pages 614–621, 1992.

[106] M. Yokoo, E. H. Durfee, T. Ishida, and K. Kuwabara. The distrib-
      uted constraint satisfaction problem: Formalization and algorithms. *IEEE
      Transactions on Knowledge and Data Engineering,* 10(5):673–685, Septem-
      ber/October 1998.

[107] M. Yokoo, E. H. Durfee, T. Ishida, and K. Kuwabara. The distributed con-
      straint satisfaction problem: Formalization and algorithms. In *IEEE Trans.
      on Knowledge and Data Engineering,* pages 673–685, Madison, Wiscowsin,
      1998.

[108] Makoto Yokoo and K. Hirayama. Distributed breakout algorithm for solv-
      ing distributed constraint satisfaction problems. In *Second International
      Conference on Multiagent Systems (ICMAS-96),* pages 401–408, 1996.

[109] Makoto Yokoo and Katsutoshi Hirayama. Algorithms for distributed constraint satisfaction: A review. In *In Proceedings of Autonomous Agents and Multi-agent Systems*, 2000.

[110] W. Zhang and L. Wittenburg. Distributed breakout revisited. In *In Proceedings of AAAI*, 2002.